Life at the ICI

Memories of Working at ICI Billingham

EDITOR: Margaret Williamson

Dedication

To the people of ICI at Billingham

Published by Printability Publishing Ltd.
on behalf of:
TEESSIDE INDUSTRIAL MEMORIES PROJECT
MAY 2008 ©

Designed and Printed by Atkinson Print Ltd.
10/11 Lower Church Street,
Hartlepool TS24 7DJ
Tel: 01429 267849 Fax: 01429 865416

e-mail: printability@atkinsonprint.co.uk
www.atkinsonprint.co.uk

ISBN 978 1872239 54 5

Contents

Preface   ix

Acknowledgements   xi

Introduction   ICI at Billingham 1919-2007 - **A brief history.**   1

Chapter   1   'Get yourself into ICI, son!' - **Starting work at Billingham.**   5

Chapter   2   'You had a responsible job to do' - **Employment at Billingham.**   16

Chapter   3   'A complex beast' - **Production.**   32

Chapter   4   'I was better for it' - **Training and personal development.**   46

Chapter   5   'They were quite strict' - **Conduct and discipline.**   54

Chapter   6   'It was paramount' - **Safety at work.**   59

Chapter   7   'Take care of the people' - **Industrial relations.**   67

Chapter   8   'Them and us' - **Relationships in the workplace.**   75

Chapter   9   'An alignment of interests' - **Benefits and facilities.**   85

Chapter 10   'Incendiaries and high explosive' - **ICI at war.**   107

Chapter 11   'No longer was there a job for life' -

                     Competition and decline.   115

Chapter 12   'A very fine company' - **Final thoughts.**   121

Appendix 1   Contributors and their dates of service at ICI Billingham.   123

Appendix 2   How ICI was organised.   124

Appendix 3   How the Billingham Site was organised.   125

Appendix 4   Map of Billingham Site c1960.   126

Appendix 5   Map of ICI Billingham and surrounding areas.   127

                     ICI Photographic Archives Collection.   128 - 140

Preface

This book contains recollections from some of the men and women who worked at ICI Billingham. It is not the definitive history of ICI, the company, but an opportunity for past employees to remember what ICI meant to them and their families. Therefore, the majority of the book consists of extracts from interviews with over 80 men and women who worked at the Billingham Site.

The people who volunteered to be interviewed came forward in a variety of ways: some responded to appeals in the local press and media; some became interested after seeing an exhibition in local libraries; others were contacted directly after recommendations from committee members and other interviewees. Whilst our contributors are just a tiny percentage of the former workforce, we are confident they represent a varied range of experiences spanning over half a century.

Our sample of interviewees held a variety of jobs, reflecting the size and complexity of the organisation at Billingham. Amongst them were process workers, craftsmen, apprentices, supervisors, engineers, technicians, clerks, secretaries, administrators, researchers and managers. They talked with pride and enthusiasm about their time with ICI. For many of them, the company was their only employer.

We have collected so many unique and vibrant memories that it has been a difficult task to decide what to include in the book and what to leave out. We did identify a number of themes that we thought would be of interest at the outset of the project and our contributors were encouraged to talk about them. I have tried to select extracts to illustrate these themes whilst also documenting the inevitable diversity of views. Editing of the interviews has been kept to a minimum and only done to improve the clarity of the book. In a few instances, this has resulted in peoples' recollections appearing to be at variance with the public records of events or processes. In these cases, I have reproduced our interviewees' versions to reflect their subjective perceptions and memories. For those who would like to examine the interviews in full, we intend to deposit recordings of the interviews and copies of the interview transcripts at Beamish Museum and Teesside Archives.

We also have included an account of the development of ICI at Billingham written by Julian Phillips and this may be useful for those who know little or nothing of its history. At the start of each chapter I have provided some relevant background information. We hope this supporting material helps when reading the experiences of our contributors.

On a personal note, I would like to thank the members of Teesside Industrial Memories Project Management Committee; Dennis Carroll, Josie Jones, Julian Phillips, Jean Richards and John Robinson. I am particularly indebted to John who has always responded immediately and constructively to my many questions. He has been an enthusiastic, efficient and tolerant guide and supporter throughout the various stages of this project. This book is the reward for all of the Committee's perseverance and hard work. It has been my pleasure to work with them.

Margaret Williamson
University of Teesside

Acknowledgements

The idea for this book was first conceived by myself, a former ICI rigger and trade union official, and John Robinson who I first met when he worked in the Personnel Department at ICI. When it became increasingly clear that ICI was leaving Billingham, we felt there should be a record of life at this once-great factory and the contribution the company made to the community, expressed through the words of people that had worked there.

Jean Richards soon joined us. Jean has never worked for ICI and brought a different perspective to our deliberations as well as a wealth of administrative skills and experience.

We decided that a wider group needed to be set up if we were to achieve our objective. This became the Teesside Industrial Memories Project (TIMP). A committee of five was elected to carry things forward, latterly comprising the three of us plus Josie Jones and Julian Phillips. The committee and three other members of TIMP carried out the interviews, giving hours of their time to carry out this vital task. We hope they enjoy the culmination of their tireless efforts.

Completing this project would have been impossible without the contribution of many people and we are delighted to acknowledge their input. Particular thanks go the people we interviewed. All welcomed the opportunity to share their vivid memories for present and future generations.

We acknowledge the enormous contribution that Dr Margaret Williamson of the University of Teesside has made to the project. She ensured that interviewers were trained to a high standard, provided much needed guidance and support as the project developed and edited this book. All this was done with great patience and good humour.

Our transcriber, Carolyn Mumford, undertook the essential, time-consuming and painstaking task of converting the spoken words into written form. Carolyn did this with great commitment for which we thank her. The contribution of Sid Field, who proof-read the manuscript, is also gratefully acknowledged.

We extend our thanks to ICI for their co-operation and encouragement. We are particularly grateful that they granted permission to reproduce official photographs. Many of these images are held in the ICI photographic archive at Beamish Museum and our thanks go to their staff who provided a professional and courteous service. In addition, we have received assistance from the staff at Teesside Archives who were, as always, generous with their time and expertise. We also appreciate the technical advice we received from Brian Liddell of Atkinson Print.

We have benefited from the support of many local organisations including Stockton Residents and Community Groups Association; Stockton Borough Voluntary Development Agency; Stockton Borough Council Museums Service; Billingham Learning Network and the University of Teesside. BBC Tees was especially helpful in publicising our activities.

Finally, we acknowledge the contribution of the Heritage Lottery Fund (HLF). The project would not have been possible without their financial support. We also thank them for their understanding and co-operation whilst we overcame a number of obstacles during the project.

We hope that the pleasure you take from reading this book is as great as the satisfaction we derived from its compilation.

Dennis Carroll
Chairman, Teesside Industrial Memories Project

ICI at Billingham 1919 - 2007
A brief history

Introduction

Most of the people recorded in this book worked at ICI Billingham between 1950 and 1980, but at least one started in the 1920s and several in the 1940s, whilst some stayed until the 1990s. For this reason the following brief account starts at the beginning and ends at the end, although the major interest is in the middle - the great technical and commercial successes of the 1960s and 1970s.

How it began

ICI's factory at Billingham grew out of the needs of the First World War. Britain's offensives on the Western Front in 1915 had faltered because of what the Minister of Munitions (later Prime Minister), David Lloyd George, dubbed 'the Great Shell Scandal'. Britain was just not producing enough TNT, the major basis for explosives. At that time natural nitrates imported from Chile were the only source that Britain had for the nitrogen (the 'N' of TNT). In Germany, however, the huge chemical company BASF had synthesised ammonia (a compound of nitrogen and hydrogen - NH3) on an industrial scale in May 1913. Thus, when the First World War broke out in 1914, the Germans already had a local source of the key raw material for making TNT. On the other hand, by 1915 British ships, and hence supplies of Chilean nitrates, were suffering from attacks by German U-boats.

This problem led Lloyd George to ask the Ministry of Munitions to set up an organisation to develop the technology to produce synthetic ammonia. Brunner Mond & Co of Cheshire was appointed to do this and chose the Site at Billingham. There is still doubt as to the reasons for choosing Billingham as the Site for the new major development although a number have been put forward. The key raw materials were readily available - coal and water. Although the anhydrite (calcium sulphate) seam was

known about, the initial plans did not include the production of fertilizers which would have needed the sulphate.

There was a completed, but as yet unused, electricity power station on Haverton Hill Road and one of the Brunner Mond directors was Sir Hugh Bell who had a major works nearby at Port Clarence and was also concerned about finding work for unemployed shipyard workers.

In 1919, however, there was a wave of rushed post-war privatisations. The Site, which was known as H.M. Nitrate Factory, actually consisted only of a few contractors' huts. The Ministry of Munitions had paid £4,250,000 for the Site in early 1918 but it was to be sold to Brunner Mond for '£715,200 more or less' according to a Ministry memorandum. They created a wholly owned subsidiary, Synthetic Ammonia and Nitrates Ltd (SA & N), to operate the Site. From this name the factory was known locally as 'the Synthetic', whilst the club that the company built for the workers was called the Synthonia Club. However, the first ammonia was not produced until Christmas Eve 1923 and by then, as it was peacetime, its major use was in the manufacture of nitrogenous fertilizers.

When Brunner Mond merged with Nobel Explosives, United Alkali, and British Dyestuffs Corporation to form the new Imperial Chemical Industries Limited (ICI) in 1926, Synthetic Ammonia and Nitrates continued as a wholly owned subsidiary. After that there was what a contemporary called 'indefinite expansion' at Billingham and by the 1930s it was the largest factory in the British Empire, employing over 10,000 people by 1930 and totalling over 1,000 acres.

More growth and the Second World War

Although fertilizer prices and sales, and hence jobs, were greatly reduced in the 1930s slump there were major new additions to the Site. The most important which opened in 1935 - also using high-pressure chemical engineering - was the oil - from - coal process. Again it was German technology, but again it was predicated on war - the next one! Britain needed a home-grown source of oil, immune from U-boat attack. Later, coal was substituted by tar from the nearby Dorman Long coke ovens. The process ran until 1958. Another 1930s development was Perspex (polymethyl-methacrylate) which, as Resin X, was invented and made in Cassel Works, and first used in aircraft cockpit covers.

So when the war came, Billingham was seen by the Government as a central industrial plank: ammonia for explosives; ammonia for fertilizers for the 'Dig for Victory' campaign; oil for high-octane fuels to enable RAF fighters to catch up with the V1 Doodlebugs and occasionally tip their wings so that they were turned around from London and crashed harmlessly into the English Channel. Billingham developed FIDO (Fog Investigation and Dispersal Operation) to clear Bomber Command's airfields in fog; and the PIAT (Projectile Infantry Anti Tank) gun with which several Victoria Crosses were won. Also, until the United States entered the war, Billingham led the UK 'Tube Alloys' project which was the code name for the development of the atomic bomb.

Billingham itself was protected by an elaborate smokescreen and a dummy factory near Greatham. It was relatively lightly bombed, and the last recorded raid was in September 1942. Nonetheless, many office departments were moved to large houses in Yarm and the outer suburbs of Stockton for the duration of the war.

After 1945 - all change

Many women had worked in the factory during the war to take the place of the men who had been called up, but when the men were demobbed they returned to their old jobs and most of the women returned to their homes. There remained industrial shortages so the factory was still working flat out. And the post-war period saw a rapid expansion in new plastics and fibres based on oil. There was no more room on the Billingham Site, so in 1945 ICI bought the larger Wilton Site south of the River Tees. Billingham Division built and ran the first olefines crackers at Wilton which broke oil into useful constituent parts. However, in 1958 there was a complete split and all the oil based interests of Billingham were hived off into the new Heavy Organic Chemicals Division.

The largest single business of Billingham remained fertilizers. Ammonia was the source of the nitrogen, and there were separate plants to produce phosphates and other essential plant nutrients, which were combined with potash into Concentrated Complete Fertilizer (CCF). The nitrogenous fertilizers were sold as Nitro-Chalk with a 15 per cent to 21 per cent nitrogen content. By 1960, however, the economics of production and of farming had changed. Ammonia production was still based on coal using the water-gas process. It was said that even if the coal were free it would have been too expensive; and farmers with better spreaders and looking for higher yields wanted a higher concentration of nitrogen. A way to use oil had to be found. The first attempt was to use heavy oil, but this proved unsuccessful. However, by 1960 Billingham had developed a catalyst to reform (literally 're-form') naphtha, a 'middle cut' of the crude oil barrel. By the mid 1960s there had been a complete technical revolution. Three new single-stream ammonia plants using naphtha roughly doubled the capacity, and halved the land and number of people used in production. The end of the coke ovens greatly reduced air pollution. At the same time a prilling process (a prill is a small round pellet) for ammonium nitrate was developed and Billingham could sell its new Nitram (with a 34 per cent nitrogen content) to farmers - less fertilizer for more yield.

The final major change started in 1970 when the plants were converted to the newly found North Sea natural gas. This reliance on local gas enabled Billingham to weather the financial shocks of the 1973 and 1979 Middle East oil crises much better than the rest of ICI, and by the end of the 1970s Agricultural Division at Billingham was ICI's major profit earner.

In 1976 ICI designed and built Ammonia 4, the only ammonia plant still operating at Billingham. It was ICI's last major investment in fertilizer production at Billingham, although a further plant was built in the 1980s at Severnside, near Bristol.

In 1971 the anhydrite mine, which had opened in 1927, was closed as the ammonium sulphate was no longer required for nitrogenous fertilizers. This led to the closure of the anhydrite-based raw meal kilns which had produced the sulphur dioxide for sulphuric acid and clinker which was ground into cement at Casebourne Works, which also closed. These combined closures saw the virtual ending of solids pollution from the Site. Similarly, when Cassel Works opened the new Monomer 8 Plant in the 1990s, 85,000 tonnes/yr of sulphuric acid which had formally been discharged into Billingham Beck was now recycled and reused.

The final years - ICI withdraws from heavy chemicals and Billingham

But all was to change, and very quickly. After half a century the world's investment in fertilizer plants was paying off in food production. The EEC had growing grain and beef mountains. The demand for Nitram slackened. And then ICI was hit by massive imports of urea (with a higher 46 per cent nitrogen content) from the USSR which was desperate to raise hard currency to feed its military responses to President Reagan's Star Wars initiative and its campaign in Afghanistan. Also, when Norsk Hydro bought the ailing Fisons Fertilisers, ICI faced real competition in its shrinking home market. Billingham's business had suffered a triple whammy.

ICI's response was to start moving away from large tonnage chemicals towards specialities and to demerge its pharmaceutical activities in 1992 to form Zeneca, now AstraZeneca. Already, in 1986 ICI had set up a new organisation based in Runcorn, Cheshire, called ICI Chemicals & Polymers (ICI C&P). ICI Fertilizers became a part of this, as did ICI Acrylics which looked after Cassel Works.

Finally, in 1999 ICI Acrylics was sold to Ineos and is now known as Lucite International. ICI Fertilizers had been sold to Terra Industries of Iowa, USA at the end of 1997. A total of 580 people were transferred, a far cry from the high point of Billingham's employment of around 16,000 in 1960. Part of this reduction was because many services such as engineering maintenance, catering, and transport were outsourced to specialist suppliers. In September 2007 it was announced that Terra and the Finnish fertilizer producer Kemira would be merging to form GrowHow UK Ltd.

Of the other plants on the Site, ICI C&P ran Oil Works until 1992 when the amines business was sold to Air Products (a US company) who closed it in 2005. The remainder of the works was sold to Cleveland Chemicals to be operated as a contract chemicals plant. It has since been bought by Dow Haltermann who still operates it. Tioxide Ltd is now Huntsman Pigments, a US company.

In the 1990s two areas of land were sold to businesses completely new to the Site; SITA who built a large energy from waste plant and a domestic recycling facility; and CPL Aromas who built a flavour and fragrance distillation facility. This has since been bought by Frutarom of Israel.

The final links between ICI and the Billingham Site were severed with the sale of ICI Eutech (Engineering) to ABB in 2001 and of Synetix (Catalysts) to Johnson-Matthey in 2002. However, ICI continued to own some parcels of land including the anhydrite mine. The company accepted a take-over offer from Akzo Nobel NV of the Netherlands in August 2007 and ceased to exist as an independent company on 2nd January 2008.

And now

The successor companies are still in place, and those who worked for ICI and built up Billingham can be proud of the heritage which they passed on to the twenty-first century.

Julian Phillips

Offices at ICI Billingham.

The majority of images and photographs in this book have been selected from the ICI photograph collection housed at Beamish Museum and grateful acknowledgement is made to ICI for permission to use copyright material.

The remaining images are credited as follows:

Pass for interview on page 11 courtesy of Stan Buglass.
Photograph of typist on page 31 courtesy of Dr Carolyn Kitching.
Photograph of Hartburn House on page 52 courtesy of Stan Buglass.
Works Rule Book on page 58 courtesy of Fred Moody.
Photograph of worker in safety helmet on page 62 courtesy of Ron Wilson.
Photograph of Research Party on page 96 courtesy of Linda Flintoff.
Long Service Award Certificate on page 100 courtesy of Barry Dunnill.
Photographs of Methanol Plant on page 120,
Queen opening the Apprenticeship School on page 137 and the LP Ammonia 3 Plant on page 140 courtesy of Barry Dunnill.
Photographs of Research Department Ladies Football Team on page 137, Research Party in 1967 on page 138 and the Intelligence Section on page 139 courtesy of Linda Flintoff.
Photograph of the New Process Offices on page 138 courtesy of Gwen Mountain.
Photograph of families visiting the factory on page 139 courtesy of Stanley Hawksfield.

Chapter 1

'Get yourself into ICI, son!' Starting work at Billingham

In 1918, when the chemical industry was first established in the area, Billingham was a village inhabited by a few hundred people but grew rapidly as ICI's operations expanded, helped by the company's reputation for providing secure employment. The wages, conditions and benefits offered by ICI were attractive and the company quickly gained a reputation as a good employer. Many of those we interviewed claimed this was their main reason for applying for a job. Our interviews also highlight the influence of family when making decisions about employment and ICI was certainly happy to recruit the sons and daughters of existing workers. Close liaison was maintained with local schools to encourage entry into apprenticeship schemes and the company developed links with universities to encourage newly trained scientists and engineers to consider a career in the chemical industry. Indeed, skilled workers were attracted to Billingham from around Britain and other parts of the world.

The first interview extracts record our contributors' feelings about joining and working for ICI. Their memories provide a suitably vivid introduction to life at ICI Billingham.

Choosing ICI: influence of family

ICI was a superb employer and all of the people inside agreed with that, otherwise they would never have stayed there. But they did stay there generation after generation. The place had started in twenty-six and anybody who worked in ICI was fighting to get their youngsters in.   (Bill Wright, 1959-1992)

My father worked at ICI. He was very glad to actually get a job there because it was one of the places which was considered really a plum place to be able to work in.

(Donald Foster, 1938-1960s)

As a schoolchild, this is during the war remember, we used to follow my father about who was in the ack-ack, Royal Artillery. We had relations down in Forest Row in Sussex and sometimes we'd go and stay on the farm there and I used to do all sorts, take the cows up onto the Downs and bring them down and follow the ploughs. I really loved it. But my father was an ex-miner, a collier, who'd had it rough as a miner in the twenties and thirties and came here primarily so that his sons wouldn't have to go down the mine. That would be round about 1930. So we ended up here and, of course, his view of work was that tradesmen were the best paid and best looked after and highest status so he said to me, 'Get a trade son.' I think at the time the company had a policy of attempting to employ the progeny of ICI employees. ICI employees who had a good reputation in the job.

(Ray Marriner, 1949-1985)

I was born and bred in Darlington so I had no long tradition of living under the shadow of ICI and knowing what it was all about. In fact, I knew absolutely nothing about it at all, to be frank. And my mother similarly, but she had heard of ICI and thought it was a good firm. 'Why don't you write to them?' And that was it. Thirty years later I'm still blaming her for that.

(Tony Brennan, 1955-1985)

I was in my last year at school. I went to a convent school in Darlington which was very strict and although, I think, my mam and dad and the teaching staff would encourage you to stay on at school, it would mean staying on at school till you were eighteen in the sixties wearing school uniform and it just didn't appeal to me at all. So mam and dad said, 'Well, if you can get a job which we approve of, we'll let you leave school after O-Levels.' So at that time ICI, of course, was the place to work and there were lots of opportunities there, different departments. I did know a couple of people who worked there so I applied to ICI to go into the Secretarial School because they paid you to train and some friends of mine left school, went to Billingham Tech and learnt how to type. I thought, 'Well, if I can go to ICI and get paid to be taught, why not? If I can get in.'

(Linda Flintoff, 1964-1976)

I was always interested in science at school but I think it was the family influence again because by then my dad had been with the firm probably twenty-ish years. My grandfather had been with the firm. I don't think I was that ambitious but I was fed up at school. Had this advert not appeared I possibly would have gone into the sixth form and by then maybe I would have thought of something else or gone on to university. I don't know but I've no doubt my dad's influence was part of that. I don't know if dad would have mentioned it. I think he thought I might have gone on into the sixth form because there was nobody in the family

The Secretarial Training School in Belasis Avenue.

At that particular time I was working for Her Majesty's Prisons and because they considered me unsuitable after a three-week period I decided to move on and the easiest way, or one of the ways, of getting into ICI was through nepotism.

(Austin Carney, 1966-1997)

In 1963/64, jobs were pretty hard to come by and my father, working in ICI for a number of years, he'd always said, 'Get yourself into ICI, son. Best place in the world.'

(Frank Curry, 1969-1985)

had been to university at that point. Maybe he thought as I was a grammar schoolboy - the first one - that it might have gone on a bit further than that. So I don't know with my dad. He had an opportunity when he was at school to have a scholarship and to go on but my grandparents couldn't afford it and he didn't get the opportunity and I think he always regretted it.

(Eric Collins, 1970-1976)

Interior of Apprentice Training School.

Choosing ICI: reputation of the company

It was the thing in those days. You know every lad wanted to get an apprenticeship in ICI when they left school.

(Stan Buglass, 1937-1980)

It was ICI and in those days to get a job at ICI was something special. Because there were so many people and it was known that they looked after their workers and their staff and you were selected. It was something very special to work there and they would look after you and the salary, of course, was a lot more than what you would get at other places.

(Jean Miller, 1952-1954)

I went there because I was sick of being educated. I thought I was sick of being educated anyway and I wanted to leave. He (father) didn't want me to go. I knew that they paid quite well and that if you wanted to advance you could.

(Jim Steedman, 1946-1987)

I knew they paid well. I'd been earning £600 a year in my last appointment as a civil engineer and I applied and succeeded in being appointed. I asked for the enormous sum of £1,000 and I got it. There hadn't been a cost of living increase for some years and a month later I got a cost of living increase of £110 so I had gone from £600 to £1,110. But I knew ICI had a reputation as being a very good employer, a reputation of giving people challenging careers. So it seemed a good bet.

(George McKinlay, 1957-1985)

Then quite by chance, I saw an advertisement in the press for ICI. It wanted personnel people with some experience. And that was quite new because ICI had, and largely continues to have had, a reputation for taking people straight from school, college, university.

But at that time ICI was doing some very exciting things in personnel management and clearly found itself short of people with personnel experience so had gone to the market place looking for people with two or three years' experience, which I'd got, to join them. I applied to join them and got the job, got the opportunity.

(John Robinson, 1969-1989)

park quite near where we lived at Raynes Park, so I said this. 'No, no,' he said and suddenly a rugby ball sort of whizzed across his desk. And as it happened, although I didn't tell him, I'd given up rugby at the age of fourteen through sheer terror and took up cross country. So I said, 'Well, I don't play much rugby, Sir,' and he said, 'ha, playing at Catterick on Saturday and we need a fly half, you look as if you'd do.'

Training laboratory assistants on the job.

The interview

When I came up to be interviewed, I'd never travelled on a first-class train before. I came overnight; I'd never travelled on a sleeper before. I was met at Darlington and was put into a huge car and was whisked through these mean little streets and I thought people would start throwing stones at us. Then taken to Norton Hall for a huge breakfast which was in chafing-dishes, and then whisked into this man's office. He looked at me and said, 'Where do you play?' I didn't really know what to say but I did play a bit of tennis and I played on a

'Oh,' I said, 'I'm going to Switzerland.' 'Do you play squash?' 'Not as such, Sir', and the whole thing was going downhill but he picked up on the Switzerland. 'What are you going to Switzerland for?' 'I'm going to climb, I'm going to climb the Dom,' which is the highest mountain in Switzerland. 'Oh, you climb, jolly good, we'll look forward to seeing you in September.' That was the end of the interview.

(Julian Phillips, 1956-1985)

I rather took them by surprise in London when I was doing my two days of interviews because it was almost like an army recruitment thing for officers and quite a thorough sort of process. At the end of it when they said that

The front of Norton Hall.

they were willing unconditionally to offer me a job in ICI and where would I be interested to work, I said, 'Well, I would be happy to work on Teesside,' because I knew the Yorkshire Moors and I knew the Yorkshire Dales and it was handy for both. They nearly fell over because their real problem was getting anyone to work in industrial Teesside.

(Robin Cook, 1961-1993)

I got into ICI almost by accident. The people who were visiting Ohio State University included ICI. I went and I put my name down to go to be interviewed by several in fact but I think the first ones who actually turned up were ICI. I had an interview with them and they offered me a job almost straight away. A group of people from ICI were on tour of the United States universities looking for people who met their requirements. It was called 'the milk round'. And I was, you know, appointed as a result of 'the milk round'.

(Keith Farmery, 1970-2000)

So I sent off an application form which my dad got for me from work. I sent that in and got a reply to go for some practical tests. They kept these tests going for years. You used to get a box, like a little tray divided into compartments. It had things like the hub of a bicycle wheel all in bits with the balls, the ball-bearings as they were then, and the bits and you had to try and put it together. You had a pair of tweezers to pick each ball up and that kind of thing. They were looking for manipulation and practical sense. I had an interview first. But then I was successful so they allocated me to instrument artificer which I'd never heard of. My dad had said, 'Get an electrician's job,' because that was the top trade, always was, I think it might still be. But instrument artificer, I thought, 'What's this?' I came along and found out what it was and I was quite happy because it involved process instrumentation which were little mechanisms that you could fiddle about with and adjust.

(Ray Marriner, 1949-1985)

I had a friend that lived opposite me and she got a job in the restaurant. So she said, 'I'll see if they want anybody.' So I was sent for an interview. It was the Grange, the old farmhouse. She said, 'A job at the restaurant? Have you ever been in a restaurant before?' I said, 'No.' She said, 'Have you been a waitress before?' I said, 'No.' 'Have you so-and-so?' So at the finish I said, 'The only thing I've had to do with food, I was once on the ice-cream counter in Woolworths.' She was looking at me up and down. I was fairly alright because I was small and slim. I got the job.

(Ellen Foster, 1950-1985)

to see me on your way back?' I called to see him on my way back and he offered me a job.

(Tony Brennan, 1955-1985)

I liked being with the Royal Insurance Company but I felt I wasn't getting anywhere and I was beginning to get bored. I wanted something a bit more. I saw an advert for a job at ICI Wilton in the paper and wrote to them for an interview and then when I told my father about it he suggested that I should write to Billingham as well, which I did, and I got an interview at both places on the same day.

The Grange farmhouse before it was bought by ICI.

I wrote to ICI and said, 'Have you got any jobs?' I was called in for an interview which I remember extremely well. I was interviewed by a guy who grilled me for quite a while and then asked me to go and see somebody in Personnel Department. When I got to Personnel Department, he said, 'Well, whilst you're here why don't you go down to the Medical Department for a medical exam and then call

The interesting thing was you had to sit an entrance test to go and when I went to Wilton we sat the test. There were about ten people there going for various jobs and we all sat the same test and the person who took us for the test went through it with us afterwards. We all had to change papers over and mark one another's papers. The strange thing was that when I got to Billingham it was exactly the same test. Except that I was on my own being interviewed and I didn't breathe a word about it. When the female welfare officer saw my paper she went down to see my father in the drawing office and said to him, 'Your daughter has done extremely well,' and I'd made my father promise not to say anything but he did then tell her what had happened. So whether they ever changed that ruling or not I don't know but I thought it was rather strange that they should have the same test at both Wilton and Billingham.

(Patricia Whyman, 1957-1964)

And I had the interview and he said, 'It'll be hard work this, being a fitter's mate.' I thought, 'I don't even know what it entails.' He said, 'Are you working now?' I said, 'Yes, I am.'

He said, 'Where are you working?' I said, 'In a bakery.' 'Oh,' he says, 'well, it's hard and heavy work.' I said, 'What do you think I do in a bakery? I just don't put cherries on top of cakes as they're going down the line.' He says, 'Well, what do you do?' I said, 'I run about with about four buckets of milk or egg or whatever, carrying four full buckets at a time and every bucket weighs thirty pounds. I'm carrying four buckets at a time, not two. I'm keeping nine machines going. I'm carrying hundredweight bags of flour and sugar and butter. I'm not frightened of a bit of hard work.' He said, 'Oh, I can see that, son. You're a nice fit young lad. Can you put your notice in and start a week or so, a week on Monday?' I did.

(Sean Booth, 1974-1994)

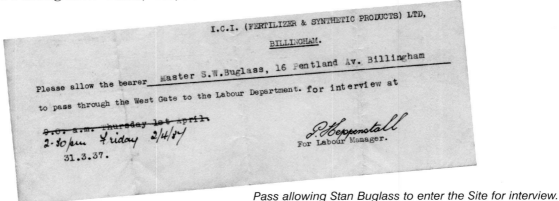

Pass allowing Stan Buglass to enter the Site for interview.

Nylon Works looking towards Middlesbrough.

West Gate with Chilton House in the background.

First impressions

It was far tidier and far cleaner and far better than the steelworks because in the steelworks you're always enveloped in smoke and filth and what have you but in ICI it all depended where you worked. At ICI there were clear roads. Splendid roads and pavements, whereas at the steelworks it was a mass of railway lines. That's why you used to have to carry all the stuff on your shoulder, on what we call a carrying stick with chain blocks on and they were heavy. But in ICI you had a handcart. If it was very, very heavy they got a tractor to take your stuff to where you were going.

(Jimmy Cutter, 1940-1978)

At first I thought, 'Oh, what have I done?' Because a gentleman that lived next door, he took me the first day and we had to go to Belasis Gate. It was pitch black and we were climbing over the railway lines and there was things happening, noises and we went through the cooling towers and, of course, they hiss when the water hits. I nearly jumped out of my skin, I thought, 'You know, it's like Dante's Inferno.' Oh, it was terrible.

(Audrey Fryatt, 1942-1945)

Walking down from the West Gate I was absolutely fascinated with the pipe bridges, the locomotives, the steam, the muck, you know, everything. I thought it was a fantastic place, I really did. And it seemed there was a buzz about it.

(Gordon Blacklock, 1953-1981)

I was at Middleton St. George in the Met. Office. We regularly used to get a phone call on a Friday afternoon from the public which was always a big event in the Met. Office because you had to make a special record in the log that you'd had an enquiry from the public. This was from a guy who was at ICI. 'This is ICI. What's the weather forecast for this weekend?' And we would tell him, give him the local area forecast for forty-eight hours and he was

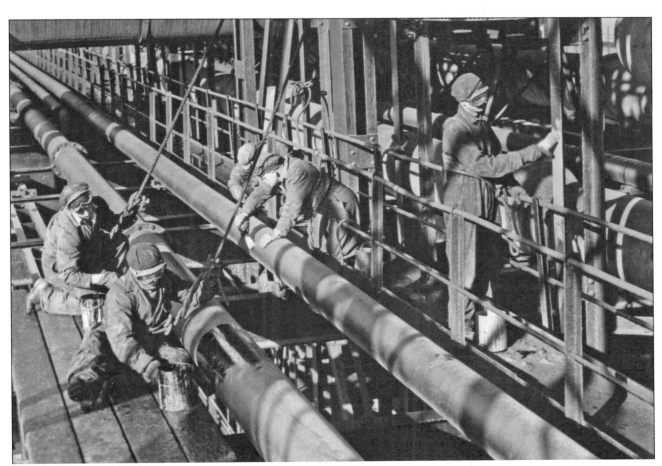

Industrial painters (brush hands) maintaining pipe bridges.

particularly interested in, 'Is it going to rain?' This went on for quite a long time and I actually began to wonder whether this was a golf enthusiast or someone who just wanted to know if he was going to get his game in. Eventually I said to him on one occasion, 'Do you mind me asking what the purpose of the enquiry is? What is it that you need to know from ICI's point of view?' And he said, 'Oh well, we need to know whether to bring the painters out to paint the pipe bridge.' My reaction was, 'But you asked me that question last week and the week before. Like how big is this pipe bridge?' Then, of course, on the day of my first interview I found out what he meant by a pipe bridge. I literally thought it was a bridge that went from point A to point B on the other side of the road to carry a pipe. When I saw the extent of how many miles of pipe bridges: the size and magnitude of that; walking past the end of number five silo and looking in through the open door and stopping aghast to discover that there was a full size dragline excavator working inside number five silo - the total impression was complete gobsmack. 'Holy smoke, this place, is incredible!'

(Tony Brennan, 1955-1985)

Then I got a surprise letter from ICI saying, 'That's jolly good, go and see one of our shows in the provinces.' So that was Billingham. In fact, with quite incredible arrogance at the time, they said, 'Look you're our sort of fast-track people. You'll probably come and run the show down here but you'd better go and run this place at Billingham.' But when I got there it wasn't like running a place at all. I was put into Distribution Department under a pair of people, one of whom had fought in the trenches in the First World War and the other had been on the Berchtesgaden raid towards the end of the war. They were real people who'd done real things and I knew nothing, as

Interior of fertilizer silo.

it were, and suddenly I was made to feel very small. At the end of the day one of these people, who had actually been a sergeant in the Air Force, said, 'Thou's had a bad day lad haven't you?' So I said, 'Yes, I agree.' He said, 'I think you'd better have a beer.' So we went to the Synthonia Club and I learnt about Newcastle Exhibition in depth.

(Julian Phillips, 1956-1985)

When I joined ICI the young graduates got what was called a Cook's tour. I can remember my first exposure to Billingham. Do you know, it was an industrial colossus and I had never seen anything like it. I thought to myself, 'How can any one person comprehend all this technology?' Because it embraces all the engineering disciplines. The physics and chemistry, it just simply embraced the lot. 'How could one person possibly comprehend this?' It was daunting, it really was. Now remember this is fifty years ago I'm talking about. I'm sure it lasted, it was at least a month and during that period we moved round all the departments, all the manufacturing, all the plants - chemical plants and so on. Again becoming more and more overawed.

(George McKinlay, 1957-1985)

The Site in 1949 looking towards Middlesbrough. The Synthonia cricket field and ICI housing are in the foreground.

Chapter 2

'You had a responsible job to do' Employment at Billingham

At its height ICI at Billingham employed about 16,000 men and women. The size and complexity of its operations ensured that they sought personnel with a wide range of skills and experience. It would surprise no one to discover that they needed chemists but they also employed other technical staff including engineers, physicists, mathematicians and metallurgists. They looked for staff to support the Site operations too. This could be in the Personnel Department (initially the Labour Department), Distribution, Sales, Supply or Payroll. Small numbers of qualified accountancy, medical and legal staff were employed and chartered surveyors worked in the Estates Department.

Skilled craftsmen such as plumbers, instrument artificers, fitters, millwrights and platers helped build and maintain the plants. But the majority of the employees in the plants were classed as process workers. There have always been small numbers of women employed at Billingham. The majority had clerical, secretarial or catering jobs but some women also worked in the laboratories and plants.

Whilst it would be difficult to cover the full range of occupations found at the Billingham Site, we have been able to include information about a wide variety of jobs. In the extracts below our contributors share their thoughts about the skills they developed whilst employed by ICI.

Computers and information technology

We had a slide rule for a lot of the time in the labs. I had a pocket slide rule for quick calculations and then I got the electric one only in about 1979/1980 and they were all new then. It was quite big. They trained us. But you had to pass the aptitude test which is to see, basically I suppose, how your mind worked and whether you would be fitted for that type of work. We all did our aptitude tests and we all passed. The other two lads went to be computer programmers and I went into computer operations which was actually running the computer. I've tried to advance myself. That was the reason for moving. But I jumped into the computer thing. I hadn't a clue what it was about. It was a promotion opportunity with more money for me and that's how I saw it and I applied for it and I got it. I hadn't a clue what I was going into. When I went from the labs into computing I could not believe it. I was completely, utterly bamboozled and the workload was staggering because in the labs you could pace yourself much better. Although we were working in the factory environment there didn't seem to be an awful lot of pressure. You just got on with your work and so on. But in the computer room you're like a driven man. You are because there are deadlines to be met, everything has to be done by morning, by this time of the day, by that time of the day. It might be the wages run on a Monday night. You know the pressure is on you. You have to get the wage slips out for the morning for the Pay Unit and all this sort of thing. I couldn't believe the sheer volume of work and although I had been a shift worker for five years by then, I started to go home off night shifts completely worn out.

(Eric Collins, 1970 -1976)

Engineers

The organisation I found in 1958 was based on the Brunner Mond version which was that you had to parallel the operators and the maintainers. Below the works manager would be a deputy works manager who I suppose you could call the operations manager and a works engineer. Then the sections. So you would have a section engineer and a section manager. Section managers were responsible for the operation of the plant, the operators, shift operators, etc. The engineers were responsible for all the maintenance work. So down that would go to the plant engineers and managers.

(Edward George, 1958-1988)

You were a plant manager and you had a plant engineer, and it was decreed that the manager and the engineer would share an office. There wasn't an engineering department and a production department. The engineer shared an office. So that when he was arranging work, maintenance of certain bits, they were there to talk to each other.

(George Morgan, 1952-1982)

Fitters

I was a fitter. As a fitter you would repair machinery, install machinery, pumps, all mechanical equipment not electrical. But you installed equipment, mended it, generally looked after the mechanical equipment on a plant. Compressors, things like that.

(Jim Steedman, 1946-1987)

In fifty-eight I went to Engineering Workshops, was placed in the millwrights and I thought that was great work. It was actually everything I wanted to do. Find faults on machines, repair the machines and get them running again. I worked in the millwrights for most of my six months stint then in the workshops. I must have shone out somehow or other because they took a shine to me and said, 'Would you like to do this as a trade? Would you like to switch over and be a millwright?' I said, 'Aye, I'm still a young lad, it seems alright to me this. I like doing this. It's very satisfying.' So that's what I did. So I did workshops then I went out

to plasterboard and gypsum, then six months in Main Offices and brought back into the millwrights. You made all your own parts. You went to lathes and machines that had broken down and found the fault, rectified the fault, got them back running again. That could be from a valve to an overhead crane, a lathe, a miller, you name it, anything mechanical the millwright would have to do it. Hydraulics, pneumatics, working on that sort of stuff as well. On occasions the little solenoid valves used to stick, 'Simpson, get yourself over here, this bloody machine's gone off again.' Because it was part of my domain - the pneumatics. I'd go across and, 'What happened last, Ralph?' 'Not bloody working is it?' 'No, what happened last, Ralph?' 'The bar came through and that was it. It's a useless damned thing!' I'd get my hammer out and just tap the solenoid and everything would work. He'd say, 'We pay you all this bloody money to hit things with a hammer!' I said, 'Ralph, you're paying for my knowledge of knowing where to hit it with a hammer, not using a hammer!'

(Roy Simpson, 1958-1999)

Instrument artificers

I've always liked hands-on. But the main thing as plant artificer you're told to look after a plant and you become a service to the process people. The first thing that any process man does if there's something gone wrong with the plant is to say, 'That reading doesn't look right to me'. So he'll say to the tiffy, 'Can you check that instrument's okay?' So you do that and you get to know the fellas and eventually they're saying, 'There's something wrong with the plant, Ray. What do you think?' And before you know where you are, you are, in fact, diagnosing with them and quite often are able to tell them what the fault can be. There's no better thing in the world to come up with a complicated situation, you move in, you do your checks and come back to say, 'I think you've got a choke in the hot catch-point valve.' Something like that. 'Oh, have you?' So they'll try something out, 'You're right.' There's no better feeling in the world than that.

(Ray Marriner, 1949-1985)

A plant control room.

Intelligence

When I was finally appointed to be intelligence manager it was very odd. I went to my group manager who spoke to me for about thirty minutes. First of all about the difference between intelligence and information, which if there is a difference, he eventually got it the wrong way round. This was a one-off job at Billingham. There was no one above me with my responsibility. The purpose of Billingham was to make and sell things. Invent, make, sell. So that any other job was not mainstream and just finding out information about things could be very important and I think it was. I was then sent to the departmental manager who rambled a bit, I thought. He didn't know either. Then he said, 'Of course, we all know this is an experiment that might fail.' So I thought that got me off to a good start. So then I went to see the [Research] Director and he said, 'There are three great libraries in the world, the British Museum, the Bodleian at Oxford, the Library of Congress - go and build the fourth.' I knew what he meant.

(Julian Phillips, 1956-1985)

Artist's impression of the new Information Centre, opened on 29 June 1979
by the Government Chief Scientist Dr Duncan Davies.

Management

I even succeeded in getting the chairman of the company to come and visit me, or visit the works. He had heard what had been achieved and he wanted to come and see for himself. I can remember him saying to me, 'There are two really good jobs in ICI. One is works manager, where you're king of the castle and the other is chairman of the company.' So I had one and he had the other. I should have said, 'I'll swap!'

(George McKinlay, 1957-1985)

I moved into Ammonia Works where the works manager thought that I ought to learn how the factory worked. The factory was a bunch of plants, ammonia plants, nitric acid plants, fertilizer plants all integrated, all linked together, really quite a complex beast. And for me to understand that was, in his mind, quite important. It was run by a particular little office called the shift managers' office which kept on top of what all the plants were doing and tweaked them a little bit and he said, 'I

think you should become a shift manager for a while and learn your way round.' So I did. I went onto shifts and I sat alongside a tried and tested shift manager, then one of the other shift managers became ill and they needed somebody to fill the slot. I nearly wet myself when I found out that I was actually going to be a shift manager for a while. I really thought, 'This is kind of pleasant to sit with somebody else while watching what he was doing.' But I ended up in the hot seat for longer than I expected. The guy was off for quite a while so I guess I must have done it for, I can't remember now, three months, six months. It was quite a while.

(Keith Farmery, 1970-2000)

Marketing

Later when developing a product called Purlboard, which was an insulation product, very expensive but very good, it meant how did you write a brochure? The next stage was finding distributors and we had a small sales force but it meant working with them and

Ammonia Works compressors. The original ammonia plant operated at very high pressure and these Peter Brotherhood compressors were made obsolete by new single-stream low-pressure ammonia plants in the mid 1960s.

going round the country and meeting people and working out what the terms were going to be. In between sixty-six and sixty-eight, we built the business up from nothing to over a million pounds a year. It doesn't seem much now but it cheered us up at the time.

However, this was insulation. We have the mildest climate of any industrial country. We virtually don't need insulation in summer because it never gets too hot and quite often it's not very cold in the winter. And, at the time, this is extraordinary to relate but true, we had the cheapest energy of any industrial country. Anyway, it was sold. You know, it's made a comeback but it would have been too long for ICI to have waited. So my marketing career went from delight at the first million to humiliation at the end.

(Julian Phillips, 1956-1985)

Medical staff

Now if you cast your mind back to the seventies and middle eighties, the whole nation was terrified of chemicals. You know, the big problem wasn't global warming, it was chemicals. Every Sunday newspaper had anxieties about chemicals and what they could do to you and so on and so forth. So a large part of my job was really to see and assess what dangers there were in chemicals and perhaps tell people what we were trying to do. Basically what we were saying was that, 'Chemicals are nasty, dangerous, corrosive and so on but we can handle them safely.' I've given lectures to Rotary and people like that and having talked about it, someone would stand up and say, 'We don't need a chemical industry, I never use any chemicals,' little realising he's got a nylon suit or Terylene shirt. There is certainly a lack of appreciation of the science and how deeply involved chemicals are in our comfort and lifestyle. I don't know whether I've ever succeeded in winning people over but there does seem to be less anxiety now. In my job remit you're perceived to be the medical expert but, of course, you can well imagine if you go out to speak to people they'll say, 'Well, you're paid by ICI so you must say this.' It really is a question of getting trust of individuals and, at the end of the day, the workers really were the best protagonists for the chemical industry because we couldn't get them if it was terribly dangerous. They said, 'Well, we've been working here for thirty, forty years and, you know, our health record is better than the average person's in Stockton.' Our mortality figures were infinitely better than the average for Stockton.

(David Bryson, 1962-1992)

People shouldn't forget that when there was an explosion on the plant, whether it was acid, ammonia or whatever, I've seen nurses pull up with their ambulance and they run like hell into wherever it was. They all got in amongst it you see, they had to, masks on, the lot. Very good service it was.

(Ron Wilson, 1960-1989)

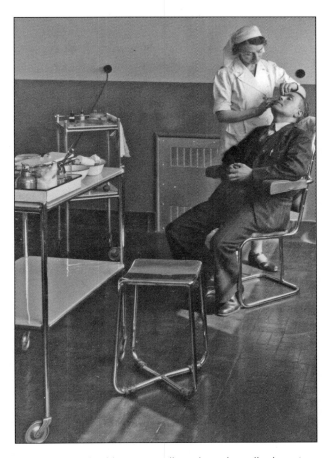

Nylon Works had its own well equipped medical centre.

Messenger boys

For two years I was the office boy at Casebourne's and did all the office boy duties that you would do in those days. Delivering the post and filing and making the tea and all that sort of thing. I used to have to cycle to the Main Offices at Billingham to collect post. The offices for Casebourne's was a set of terraced houses joined together in one on the main road opposite the factory which produced the cement and it was fairly thriving in those days, as far as I recall. I thoroughly enjoyed that time. You were busy; you had a responsible job to do.

(Stan Buglass, 1937-1980)

When you started work as a messenger boy you had to go on a training course. You learned how to knock on office doors, how to answer telephones, how to take messages, how to perform in other people's lives. You got points deducted if you had dirty fingernails or your tie wasn't straight. We were all put into teams, we all had a different coloured badge and at the end of each week they said who was top of the leagues and who's not top of the leagues and you had an inspection every morning before you started work. So it was quite a hard regime for someone leaving school.

(Roy Simpson, 1958-1999)

assembled them down there. They had a loco down there. As my dad used to say, 'Billingham will have the best, deepest, widest, deep-sea harbour in the world one of these days because the factory will set off and collapse.' Now that has never happened and I don't suppose it ever will.

(Fred Moody, 1946-1982)

This view of the anhydrite mine shows the very large machinery that could be used in the mine.

Miners

People call it a mine but it was an underground quarry really. A very dear friend of mine got permission to go and have a look at it. Of course, he was astounded. Canteen and picture house and God knows what. Enormous vehicles and trains running about. They assembled them down the bottom. Came in crates, put them down the shaft and then

The charges were placed and they were fired, of course. If they didn't fire you had a broken lead which you tested on your battery and the ohmmeter gives you a circuit. So you could tell if it was broken. Then you'd go in and find the broken wire or if it hadn't been connected properly repair it, come back out, fire the place and then when you went back in to test for gas. You tested for gas before you charged, you tested for gas after you charged and you tested for gas after you'd fired. Then you would find a misfire or misfires. Now the routine was to come out, fence it off and wait 'X' number of hours. I don't know if it was thirty minutes or something like that. You'd go in, test them, run your wires out to a safe place, test them again and then go in and remove them. If you could remove them you took them out. You made your sheet out. It went in the book. The Government Mines Inspector's book. All the detonators you drew and the detonators you returned all recorded in the Mines Inspector's book.

(Thomas Green, 1953-1991)

Personnel

And the job of the personnel officer on the works was the focal point of a generalist approach. We had a huge array of specialised personnel functions. There was the Monthly Staff Pay Unit, the Weekly Staff Pay Unit, the Weekly Staff Welfare System. The canteens, the job assessment scheme, weekly staff assessment, monthly staff assessment, working conditions payments. All of that lot had their own little specialists in Personnel Department.

A miner preparing for shot firing. The anhydrite mine had much higher galleries than most coal mines.

The joint consultation system, retired employees summer outings, everything was done in Personnel Department. The personnel officer on the works was the sole contact on that works for any of those subjects and a few more besides. We always used to reckon that ICI employed an expert in every single field. Like in the days of 17,000 employees on the Site we had every occupation from a pastry cook to a blacksmith, from a sign writer to an optician. They were all there. Whatever your problem was, you could find an expert somewhere but if you ever came up with a problem that you couldn't find an expert for, you gave it to personnel. And that's where the personnel officer was the front man. In terms of a day in the life of a personnel officer, job assessment was always great fun. The monthly staff job assessment, Haslam Scheme, was always producing managers chuntering because their lads wanted more money and couldn't I fiddle it for them and presenting a wonderful case as to why I should fiddle it for them and me saying, 'On your bike and go away.' Then they'd go away and write up a job description and bring it back and you'd send it back with, 'Is this the script for the next version of the Goon Show?' We had a lot of fun with that. It was really not in my hands because I was holding the balance between the management on one hand and my expertise behind me in the assessment co-ordination outfit who would make sure that nobody got away with blue murder. But if the results came back, the personnel officer would have to sit down with the manager in charge of that incumbent to discuss how that would be applied, what the salary treatment would be, whether he'd actually already been doing that job for a length of time as described. I also had to pick up and try to regularise the whole of the assessment history for the works. I actually finished up doing a lot of work just simply to get a card index system going that recorded every job that had ever been assessed on the works.

(Tony Brennan, 1955-1985)

One of the things that we had to do as fairly new labour officers, we had to go out and assess abnormal conditions. This was a scheme where if an employee was asked to do a job which was beyond what they would normally expect, then there was a scheme whereby a labour officer could go and assess an extra payment for that job to be done. And so you felt in a way you were playing a part from early on with that but, of course, unions didn't always agree with what you were coming out with. But you had to keep a sense of proportion and that did bring you face to face with the employees who were doing really difficult jobs. At Billingham, for example, in the Sulphuric Acid Plant you were climbing into spaces only eighteen inches high to work on lead which was, of course, poisonous. And so again the confined space of that was quite scary. Some people with claustrophobia couldn't have done it, so again that would carry a payment.

(Robin Cook, 1961-1993)

Planners

Overhauls Group was the most enjoyable time I had in my life because I was more or less my own boss. Engineers and managers allow you to project yourself if you knew your job. We were told there was a shutdown on, you'd go down and plan the job. 'We'll leave you to it,' because you've got a certain amount of time to do it, so many jobs and I just went and did it. But then I developed into what you call a multi-trade planner and I, again not to be smug or anything like that, turned out to be what I consider one of the best because I had this certain flair inside me and I wanted to succeed and be good. So I turned out to be respected, I think. Anyway, I must have been because I was sent down to represent the Overhauls Group at Castner-Kelner Works in Runcorn.

(Barry Dunnill, 1956-1994)

Process operators

The person that was training you would say, 'Oh well, we have this level and we've got the valve here and we move the valve up and down to keep that level straight. Right, fair enough, that's a simple explanation.' Most of the stools were three-legged stools that you sat and watched these levels on. The amusing thing was when you asked these people, 'Well, what's this level?' They would look at you and say, 'Well, it's a level, it's liquid, you know, that's why it's a level.' And you would say, 'Well, what's the liquid?' They really didn't know whether it was water, sulphuric acid or brine or petrol or anything. They just didn't know what it was. All they knew was they sat there and they kept this level by moving the valve. Hand control. Believe it or not when you went to Cassel Works where they made explosives, it was the same system. Primitive, absolutely, primitive. There were 21,000 people working at ICI when I first started. In the Phosphate Plant where they crushed the phosphate rock that came from Morocco and such as that and crushed it and put it in a mill, literally people sat and watched the bunker level when it went. Sat on the edge of a bunker. They might have five bunkers to walk up and down but that's literally what they did. They walked up and down a bunker saying, 'Oh, we want some more stuff in so-and-so bunker.'

(Fred Moody, 1946-1982)

The cell room in Cassel Works where brine was split into sodium and chlorine.

Mostly you were working on the instrumentation. There wasn't only me, there were a few lads like me had done it by hand and were curious as to why we were doing it by hand. They'd found out what the damned stuff was and what it was doing and where it was going to and where it was from. There was a few of us, there wasn't just me. Because of the automation and control rooms and the blocker panels we wanted to know what the hell's this thing doing. The instrument. What is it doing? Why is it there? What's it telling us? We used to go out on the plant and find out, even if it was only just where the product was. Where was it taking the temperature from? I always wanted to know where it came from. In later days when I was a chargehand and foreman I used to always say I'd got a process man when a bloke turned round to me and said, 'Why?' When they started the process youth system up and I got involved with that I never used to say much to them. I used to tell them what was the job was doing, how it was run and what we were running it for. Where it came from and where it went to. But when the lad turned round to me and said, 'Why?' I knew I had a process worker.

(Fred Moody, 1946-1982)

My role initially was finishing operator. It was analysing the crystals, determining whether they would be in a position where they could dry properly. Then you moved on to what they call 'up the tower' because the guy who was up the tower wouldn't be up there for eight hours, he would be bored out of his mind. Because he would switch over. It would be his turn to do the analysis and the person at the top of the tower would then look after the prilling of the urea. At Nylon where one of the first jobs I did before going on to shifts, an engineer came along and he said, 'Right, I need you to look at the salt pump and I don't want the salt to rise above the sight glass. If it does I want you to operate this valve here to bring the salt back down again and it is just a combination of nitrogen and air.' Then I thought, 'Well, what happens if it does go over the pipe work - this salt. Is it going to wreck the pump, or if this air goes down is it going to push the product back down?' He never really told me that. It's just a matter of controlling the salt level.

(Austin Carney, 1966-1997)

People really underestimated processors because they were called general workers.

(Dennis Carroll, 1952-1979)

Research

I worked totally in the Research Department, Physical Chemistry - I suppose you'd call it - Department. The Catalyst Section. We were dealing just with catalysts. The biggie in those days was the development of vanadium pentoxide as the catalyst for turning SO_2 into SO_3 for the Sulphuric Acid Plant. Testing everything and now, of course, it's standard issue in school textbooks, vanadium pentoxide. But it was, 'Shush don't tell anybody,' at that time. A big industrial secret. Now, for example, we were testing various ways of presenting this vanadium pentoxide to reaction and since it was powder coated very, very thinly on another chemical, in my area silica gel, it would tend to blow away in the reactor with gases passing through it. So they decided it would be in pellet form and we went off to this pelleting machine, hand-operated pelleting machine and we made hundreds of pellets of different power settings and different pressure settings. Then they would go back and you would run them through the test rig and then the most promising things from that were run through the pilot plant. All the time you were gaining knowledge. This was first-principle research. Then developing on from that and they eventually selected what seemed to be the best and you made a large amount of pellets for the pilot plant. Automatic pelleting machines somewhere would churn out all these pellets so you wouldn't have to do each one individually by hand. They were running on the old methods and we were obviously trying to develop an almost revolutionary new one. Vanadium pentoxide is a lot cheaper than platinised asbestos which was the old catalyst. That used to poison and then they had to stop the whole plant and take out all the platinised asbestos, put new stuff in and, of course, you can imagine what that cost.

(Allan Wilderspin, 1953-1955)

Post-war Research and Development buildings with Engineering Department huts in the foreground.

He was rather eccentric in many respects but what a brain, what a remarkable brain. I think he had two double firsts from Cambridge in chemical engineering and mechanical engineering and he was a man who delved into what we called fundamental research. It was research that had never even been dreamt of before and I happened to get seconded to him so he and I became a sort of a team. He did all the thinking and I did all the work. And it was remarkable because he used to come in the morning. He had always been thinking about some particular formula which he had been developing and he wanted to test it in the laboratory. So we would sit down and develop some form of apparatus to develop this theory which he'd dreamt up and we would work and we would work and we would work. Some of the designs of the apparatus we were dealing with were quite fascinating really. Never been done before and the work that we were doing was so complex it lost me. It was so theoretical.

(Alf Illingworth, 1952-1969)

Riggers

I didn't know very much about rigging but I'd seen them working and I thought, 'Well, it looks dangerous that,' but they were an important part of the ICI set up because they were an integral part. They were the first to go on a job and the last to come off and they were in the middle of it. Basically a rigger has the ability and the training to move and lift heavy weights, in simple terms. The scaffolders put scaffolding and tubing up and, of course, we had to learn how to do that in a very minor sort of way. The more I talked to them the more I was interested because they were on good pay then compared to me. But they put a lot of hours in and they worked maybe two, three nights and then Saturdays and Sundays.

(Dennis Carroll, 1952-1979)

I liked building new structures. I liked working with platers and them more than fitters really because it was hands-on. You got your toggle and you got it all ready to get the bolt in and it was very interesting work. Then when you finish it was like a Meccano set, you were building a Meccano set. There was something at the end of it there what you'd actually done. Not just you, the team, the team itself.

(Hughie Norman, 1958-2005)

We had to work out in all weathers. Our foremen used to say, 'Come on, let's have you outside, your skin's waterproof.' You had to get out because you were doing the job and you had to get out.

(Brian Rodgers, 1957-1987)

Riggers at work.

Telephonist

At night, at five o'clock, you would switch lines over to the [factory] fire station. They took the first five incoming lines and there would be other lines that were pinpointed through the Site. First of all, you would take those lines down and then you would begin to take the calls. Now in the early days, well even in 1978, we still used what you called 'private wires'. Those were dedicated lines, telephone lines to other sites - Wilton, Runcorn, Welwyn, Slough, Winnington. So you would have dedicated operators to do 'private wires' so if anyone came through and said, 'I want a call to Runcorn Heath please,' we would make a docket out, pass it down to the operator and she would book it. We would say, 'Yes, we'll call you back,' and if they say, 'well, it's rather urgent.' 'Well, there's only one waiting but, if you like, if it's that urgent we'll put it in front.' So those were private lines. From 1961 till at least 1978 all the calls basically had to come through the switchboard. All the local calls, trunk calls and the 'private wire' calls and, of course, we had started by then dialling internationally, to ring Moscow and America and things like that. I grew up with that because it started off while I was on the telephones in London in the fifties where gradually we started ringing outside of London instead of getting an operator. Then by the time I had come to Billingham you could dial national numbers and then America. I remember one time we were told we could ring America and this was the dialling code. This was while I was at Cassel Works so we thought, 'Right, we're going to try it.' We had the dialling code so we made up the rest of the number. We didn't know who we were ringing and the number rang out and this person said, 'Hello, hello there, hello,' and we said, 'oh, sorry to disturb you, we're just testing a line to America.' 'That's okay but do you realise what time this is?' We had completely forgotten about the time zone. Then we got a new system in the early eighties and that was an American solid-state electronic system. Then everything changed. By then the teleprinters had changed from keying out a code number to being put into a computer. So messages were going via the operator into the computer, storing them into the computer. The new telephone system did away with the old-fashioned plug-type switchboard. Communications budget was four million pounds a year. That usually was split up into the usage of the departments and we would charge them for using the facilities - telephones and teleprinters - but now the new equipment had come in we were getting less and less usage through the departments. And, of course, we were getting less and less calls through the switchboard so we needed less. So come about eighty-eight, eighty-nine, we had very few calls through the switchboard. ICI then was starting to thin down and to cut things. And departments were bringing what we called the 'axemen' into the departments, thinning them out and everything.

(Rita Stafford, 1961-1991)

Trainers

I went into Engineering Department and that would be in forty-seven. I stayed in Engineering Department as a draughtsman until fifty-one. I got transferred to Education Department. The messenger boys used to come in and spend a week on an induction course and the various training officers had to be temporary leaders of a group of these lads, about four teams and you sort of sponsored them. Then in 1956 I went to see the then education officer and I went to Norton House at Hartburn. There I did foremen's training courses primarily. Originally did some estimator training and work study training but primarily I was involved with the foremen's training course which then was twelve weeks if I remember rightly. There was one week on the course and two weeks off. We used to set them homework and other things. They were very, very good. Very demanding because these foremen candidates were of various age ranges, some with a lot of experience, some with little. And an ideal place for the training. We had our own dining facilities and everything there. During the break times we even played croquet.

(Stan Buglass, 1937-1980)

I was asked to apply and I was appointed adult instrument training instructor to look after all the adult courses. You just keep going and when a new instrument comes in they run a course and you learn about it. I didn't have any trouble with the adults but I hadn't been leading that too long when I took over from my boss who was the instrument electrical training officer and looked after all of them because he was going off to Malaya to an ICI plant out there. So once you get in amongst apprentices, lads being lads, they sent up cheek to what they would regard as petty officials. I always remember one with a time-keeper. We were off site so we didn't have to go and get our pay slips at work - in the Training Centre that is. A man would come there and bring the stuff over. He would also come over during the week and check off time keeping figures and he used to have to stand there and these lads would be waiting for their pay slips. He would dish them out and if they weren't in the right mood or if he said something, because he could be a bit acid himself, some of the lads might react. There were a couple of lads, brothers they were, one of them ended up taking my job over in the Training Centre several years later funnily enough, and they said they'd set their lip up to him. So I checked with him first, he'd made his complaint and checked with the lads and they more or less agreed that they had been insolent, shall we say. They were fairly young at the time. So I had to call them in and we decided that we would write a report and put it in the records, nothing further than that, just this incident is reported and is described. Put it in the records. Next thing I know I get a phone call, 'Mr Armstrong wants to come and see you.' I said, 'Who's he?' 'He's so-and-so's dad,' the two of them. So he came up and he was irate with me. 'You can't do this with my boy. They said it was his fault.' I said, 'I know but he's the bloke in charge and anyhow it's not a serious thing. It will go on the records and come off again in a couple of years if they have no further trouble.' Anyhow, he was placated. So that's the kind of thing you get involved with.

(Ray Marriner, 1949-1985)

Apprentice Training School.

Typists and secretaries

This was a vast office of girls doing nothing but type all day. The noise, I can't describe to you what a culture shock it was from going from a schoolroom to this office. It was in two halves, one half with the shorthand typists and the other half with the copy typists, who did things like invoices and mundane stuff as that. The shorthand typists worked for the men in the department, mainly the section managers and took their shorthand and typed their letters and everything. It was overseen by two dear little ladies. But we never addressed them by their Christian names, it was always 'Miss' and we were referred to as 'Miss' all the time. You didn't get familiar and, of course, all these typewriters. I am just trying to think how many there would be. Maybe thirty. It was a big, big room and the noise, can you imagine thirty manual typewriters clack, clack clacking away? You weren't allowed to do things like talk. If you did speak to somebody else it was purely business and it didn't last very long. The gimlet eye of the supervisor would be watching you. Even things like excusing yourself to go to the ladies. You couldn't just get up and go, you had to go and say, 'Please may I leave the room?' But very, very regimented and if you lingered too long she'd send somebody to see where you were. It was unbelievable, unbelievable.

(Rita Nicholson, 1948-1966)

We were all called secretaries but I should think that now they'd be called PAs because the stuff we did was amazing. We did, for example, a tour of the plants and he would say to me when he was going to be doing a tour of the plants so I'd nip and talk to the section manager or engineer and say, 'You know he's coming next week, you get that plant sorted out and you know you're not making your targets. You know you've got to make this.' And that sort of thing. So we did, you know, lots of things that were all part and parcel of the business.

(Brenda Fuller, 1963-1967)

I always used to say that being a secretary was a little bit like being a housewife. You had to look after the men.

(Patricia Whyman, 1957-1964)

I remember once the phone went and I went and answered it. It was a man and he said, 'Is the manager there?' I said, 'No.' 'Who's that?' he said. 'Oh, it's just one of the typists.' He said, 'Never run yourself down like that, dear. You're not just one of the typists.' I can remember that to this day.

(Patricia McNerney, 1945-1949)

Typist in the Secretarial School.

Chapter 3

'A complex beast' Production

When the Government first decided to build a plant at Billingham, it was to provide synthetic ammonia for the explosives needed during the First World War. Ammonia and ammonium sulphate were produced at the Site from 1923 initially under the auspices of the Brunner Mond Company. The capacity for producing ammonia increased substantially when ICI was formed in 1926 and shortly afterwards they also began to diversify their product range. An anhydrite mine was opened at Billingham in 1928 and this was used in the manufacture of cement in the nearby Casebourne Works. Methanol production was also started in 1928, followed early in 1929 by the start of production of a new fertilizer, Nitro-Chalk, a combination of ammonium nitrate and chalk. Concentrated Complete Fertilizer (CCF), a mixture of nitrogen, phosphorus and potassium, began to be manufactured at Billingham in 1930. In the same year, a new factory, originally named Billingham South Works and later renamed Cassel Works, began to produce chlorine, caustic soda, sodium and cyanide.

The early 1930s was a difficult period for ICI commercially. The company found marketing the new fertilizer products problematic and demand was decreasing. At the height of the depression between 1929 and 1931, it is estimated the workforce at Billingham fell by about 6,000. ICI once again responded by increasing diversification. The manufacture of Drikold, dry ice, began in 1932 and urea production started in 1935 both using carbon dioxide, a by-product of ammonia manufacture. They also opened a plant to produce petrol from coal in 1935 and a small plastics plant which developed Perspex.

In the years following the Second World War, the demand for products manufactured at Billingham increased and they continued to produce large amounts of fertilizers, ammonia, Drikold, cement, methanol and sulphuric acid. At this point Billingham was the largest chemical complex in the world. During the subsequent years, technological advances improved productivity and capacity but essentially the Site at Billingham continued to concentrate on the production of inorganic chemicals.

Our contributors describe working in the following factories at Billingham: Ammonia Works; Casebourne Works; Cassel Works; Nylon Works; Oil Works and Products Works. Ammonia Works made ammonia, methanol, carbon dioxide and urea. Casebourne Works produced cement, plaster and plasterboard whilst Cassel Works produced sodium, cyanide, caustic soda and chlorine. Nylon Works was responsible for the manufacture of nylon polymer; Oil Works produced petrol and a wide range of organic chemicals and Products Works manufactured fertilizers, sulphuric acid, nitric acid and other ancillary products. In the following selection of extracts the people who managed and worked in these plants and processes explain the technical aspects of their jobs and present an atmospheric glimpse into a world unknown to the majority of us.

Descriptions of the Billingham Site

I went to at least twenty plants, maybe more than that. From the mine to power raising, to steam raising, to ammonia production, to methanol production. It was just non-ending and you used to go from one particular group because a lot of the ICI design was such that it was set aside in different groups depending upon the work that they undertook. There was gas and power, there was electrical generation. There was the mine which was a separate one. There was Casebourne's that produced cement. There were other ones that produced ammonia and methanol and a whole range of industrial chemicals.

(Mansell Shotton, 1942-1984)

Apprenticeships in 1949, when I started with ICI at Billingham, lasted for five years. My five years began in a small Engineering Training Centre which had been the old gun shop during the war of 1939-45. After learning basic hand tool and machine skills I went into the main workshops, on light instrument construction and repair. I also had a month in

the heat-treatment shop, learning about hardening steel components. By this time I was into my second year and transferred onto Oil Works into the plant instrument maintenance shop, for my first real view of plant conditions and chemical process control and measurement. What a change: Oil Works was an old works whose early products were petroleum fuel produced from powdered coal. Everything smelt of oil. It was a no-smoking zone naturally because of the risk of fire on almost every plant. There were small smoke huts dotted in safe places, with electrically heated coils to light your smokes. As a beginning, I was allocated to a tradesman who was working on the construction of a new acetone plant; the work being mainly fitting and installing thermocouples and cables. It was clean work being physically separate from the older parts of the works. As time passed I was allowed more freedom to work unsupervised.

Aerial view of Billingham Site in 1982. At this stage it was the largest, single, private producer of ammonia in the world with four ammonia plants.

This, of course, was great and busy but obviously more satisfying, knowing it was 'real work'. This, plus a short time on the plants repairing instruments, filled my eight months in Oil Works. Next I was posted to Cassel Works, another collection of old processes, most of which were very dusty and unpleasantly smelly. For instance, cyanide, hydrochloric acid, chlorine and sodium, where the process men seemed to spend all their time wandering along rows of pots containing sodium under heat and poking through the vents to allow the liquid sodium to flow out. They were completely covered in leather protective clothing, with leather helmets; that plant was like something out of hell! One plant, relatively new was quiet and laboratory-like with sections of the plant encased in glass-walled rooms. Entry in there was allowed only if gloves and a compressed-air mask were worn and someone must be at all times observing you. That product was HCN (hydrocyanic acid) - fatal as gas or liquid on the skin. This, of course, was incredible, but I was allocated to an old tiffy who had been gassed in World War One, who could not exert himself at all. This was great for me, as having shown I was keen, he taught me lots of things about instruments of many types - again satisfying working on my own more and more. The smell of leaking chlorine and hydrochloric acid takes your breath away, grabs your throat and stops your breath. I soon learnt to sniff - if gas was present, hold my breath and walk towards the plant's limit, sniff again and repeat till the sniff revealed you were clear of the gas. I had eight good months there and was developing skills, knowledge and confidence in the on-line maintenance of process instrumentation.

The Portrack fertilizer complex with the CCF and two Nitram plants in the foreground.

Next was Nylon Works. This works, with the exception of the Adipic Acid Plant, was very clean and extremely tidy, being a pretty new works. The Instrument Shop was very organised and most tradesmen were twenty to thirty-five years of age. By this time I'd had lots of experience over the range of processes and the instruments which measured and controlled their product manufacture. After the precision and organisation of Nylon, I was moved to Products Works, most of whose plants were designed to manufacture a range of synthetic fertilizers, e.g. CCF, sulphate, sulphuric acid, nitric acid, nitrates. The acid plants were smelly and dusty, being relatively old, the rest were just old and dusty. I only had one more plant to go to before I completed my apprenticeship - Research Works, which was a miniature version of other works constructed in and around laboratories. Clean, small-scale and we all wore dustcoats! By now we were treated like tradesmen and left to get on with the work tasks allocated to us.

(Ray Marriner, 1949-1985)

Shipping bagged fertilizers.

We made fertilizer because in those days there was a shortage of food worldwide and it was the Government, I think, that instigated the need to create man-made fertilizer rather than rely on cows and horses and, in essence, we were shipping it worldwide. India was one of the biggest users of our product but also all the farmers in England used it. Well 99.9 per cent. It was all bulk fertilizer to get as many crops as they could and healthy crops. And, in that sense, that's what we were there for and that's what we did because production in farms clearly was better with the fertilizer than without it. So that was our goal but, of course, making fertilizers is a dirty business. It's smelly. You needed ammonia and you needed sulphuric acid, nitric acid fumes floating over the horizon. You know, that awful brown plume you could see. That's one of the consequences and, of course, the river was getting polluted because the effluent was just going into it. So that was what we were there for. They didn't only make fertilizer. We made nylon, of course, which was a money-spinner. We made plastics, we made ammonia. During the war they made plastic for the aeroplanes and there was some work going on up in the Research Works on the atomic bomb. We didn't know that, it wasn't called that. They used to have another fancy name for it.

(Dennis Carroll, 1952-1979)

Ammonia Works

I think it speaks volumes the length of time I spent on Ammonia 4. And I had no qualms. It was challenging. Something different. Anything that had to be shut down was shut down properly in the right procedure. So yes, everything was challenging. I was comfortable with it and enjoyed my time there. Between the LP Ammonia 1, 2 and 3 and Ammonia 4, there was a little bit of competition. It was because Ammonia 4 saw themselves as blue-ribboned.

(Austin Carney, 1966-1997)

Ammonia 4 Plant in 1977, the last major fertilizer-related investment at Billingham.

Billingham realised that they were (and should have realised it earlier frankly) way behind technically with a process based on coal. So they had developed the pressure steam reforming process and decided to put four plants at Billingham and two at Heysham, these replacing the coke ovens, the Coke Oven By-product Plants, the Water Gas Shift Plants and the low-pressure compressors. It is my view that it probably cut out 17,000 tons of coal a year and also led to the closure of coal mines in Durham. The feedstock for this was naphtha which is best described as low grade petrol. The Steam Reforming Plant consisted first of all of a little sub unit called the Howe-Baker Plant which was there to take sulphur out of the naphtha. It used concentrated sulphuric acid to do that. It then went to the Steam Reforming Plants, was vaporised and passed to a further de-sulphurisation process. Mixed with steam, it passed down forty-foot long four-inch diameter tubes in a furnace. From the bottom of the tubes came hydrogen plus carbon monoxide which passed to the secondary reformer. Into this air was introduced, so that you ended up with hydrogen, nitrogen and, of course, carbon dioxide, carbon monoxide and residual steam. That gas was then fed back into the original Ammonia Works, IP compressors in T2 building. So it did away with the whole of the coke ovens and all that complex.

(Edward George, 1958-1988)

The raw synthesis gas, which is a mixture of hydrogen, nitrogen, carbon dioxide (CO_2) and carbon monoxide (CO), used to be produced from reacting coke with steam and air. In the 1960s the basic feedstock became naphtha. The raw synthesis gas was then produced by steam reforming of naphtha over a special catalyst, manufactured by ICI, to produce hydrogen, followed by air addition to add the nitrogen. The raw gas then had to be purified by removing the carbon dioxide and the carbon monoxide. To remove the CO_2 the raw gas went to the CO_2-Removal Plant. This building contained many water wash towers, which were used to scrub the CO_2 out of the raw gas. After that in the CO-Removal Plant, in a separate building, the CO was removed by scrubbing the raw gas with copper liquor.

After that, once again in a separate building, the now purified gas would go to the Synthesis Plant, where the hydrogen and nitrogen in the correct 3:1 ratio were reacted over a catalyst in high-pressure reactors. The ammonia gas produced would then, in another building, be liquefied by refrigeration, and then put into storage. Ammonia cannot be stored as a gas so it has to be liquefied. On single-stream plants all these processes are done on one plant, which takes up a much smaller area.

(Doug Wallace 1957-2000).

So, for example, in Billingham there were ammonia plants which turned, basically, air and water and natural gas into ammonia, or into methanol. Well, you can't do that in your kitchen, it has to be made in a very sophisticated process. Inside that process are very, very high technology materials called catalysts which actually turn synthesis gas into ammonia, or into methanol or into various other things. And that was the reason the department was there. The factory had three or four ammonia plants. It had methanol plants. That was its business. It needed to be very, very good at making those products and so it therefore needed to understand the catalysts which were at the heart of the process and so it did a lot of research in that area and indeed it sold those products all round the world. So if you have an ammonia plant or a methanol plant and it's in India or Australia or Canada there's every chance that the catalyst that would have been in there would have been designed, developed by the research people at Billingham. A major global business. Was then, still is. Supplies 40 per cent to the world's industry, I would suspect. Yes, the world would be a different place without the catalysts made at Billingham.

(Keith Farmery, 1970-2000)

I was asked to go on to Ammonia 4 Plant. This was a brand new plant designed by ICI. It was commissioned at the end of 1976. I went on the plant as plant manager in January 1977. I missed the commissioning. There had been a commissioning team, which then moved off the plant and left the basic team to run the plant. Compared to the 1966 Kellogg LP Ammonia Plants, Ammonia 4 Plant was a totally different ballpark. The plant was wonderful. It was designed by ICI, started up by ICI people and it ran like an absolute dream. It was not like the old 1966 Kellogg Ammonia Plants. A very significant change happened in 1971. Up to 1971 all the ICI ammonia plants used naphtha as the main feedstock. In 1971 North Sea natural gas (mainly methane CH_4) became available. So from 1971 all the ICI ammonia plants were converted to use natural gas instead of naphtha as the main feedstock. To convert the plants was a major operation.

After the conversion it was so much easier to run the plants because methane is a gas and made the plants a lot easier and safer to control. For example, as naphtha is a liquid it had to be pumped and there was an additional section of plant to vaporise the naphtha liquid before it was used. Also steam reforming of methane (CH_4) which is a 1-carbon compound is a lot easier and more controllable than naphtha (C_7H_{16}) which is a 7-carbon compound.

(Doug Wallace 1957-2000).

Ammonia 4 Plant in 1977, the last major fertilizer-related investment at Billingham.

Casebourne Works

I worked in Casebourne's on the hair plaster and cement. That was a fascinating job - hair plaster. You got the plaster raw from the kilns and you had bags of goats' hair from Morocco. And you put so much hair to so much plaster and so much dye to it there. I think it was the only time in ICI I ever used grams.

(Fred Moody, 1946-1982)

I had to report to the Plasterboard Plant and I worked there for two or three days and then the chargehand up there says, 'Oh, they want you to go to the Cement Plant.' So I went down to the Cement Plant and I stayed there, I can't remember how long. It was not long after the war and much was going on. They were building more silos and they were building a control unit. And the control unit was actually in the crushing plant.

It went into a screw device like a mincing machine and it passed the cement into what they called Fluxo bottles. When they were full there was a sensing device that shut the cement going in and then the compressed air was blown in and it blew the cement up through pipes into the silos.

(Stanley Hawksfield, 1950-1978)

Cassel Works

I actually got an interview in Cassel Works for this job as general foreman for civil squad or whatever you want to call it. I went across to Cassel Works, did the interview, had a walk round, they offered me the job and I took it. In charge of what they called a day squad. At that time it would be about twenty, I think. I was the foreman for day services. Completely different type of work, area of work, site smells, the lot.

Loading bags of cement at Casebourne Works.

Lots of chemicals. Cyanides, methacrylates, you name it, I think it was in that area. So it was a complete change of work.

(Bill Smith, 1964-1998)

When I joined they said, 'Oh, the Cyanide Plant won't last long.' This was in seventy-four and it's closing this year. On that plant everything was behind walls and windows. At the top it was a one, two, three or four storey plant, with floors on each level. At the top of the plant on the roof there were some fans which drew air up. We used to call them cubicles; push the air out of the top so if there were any leaks it all went out of the roof. I remember once that one of the fans stopped. There was a remote 'clunk' and then a sort of silence amongst the rest of the sound. There was one particular sound missing. And one of the more experienced chaps said, 'Oh, the fan's gone,

we'd better get out.' Because at that stage the air's not being sucked inside the cubicles it's allowed to go out. We used to take risks. To go inside the cubicle you were supposed to get a .....was it neoprene? Sort of a flexible diver's type suit on to completely cover your body. Put wellington boots on with the trousers over the boots and put a breathing set on and fully cover your face once you'd got a breathing set on. You'd have to get kitted up, plug the air in for an air supply, have somebody standing at the door watching you and you'd go in and open up a couple of the valves which would take about thirty seconds. Unless a manager or a supervisor was around. Even supervisors knew what we did. We'd just open the door, hold our breath, dash in and dash out again. I wouldn't do it nowadays.

(Christopher Snowdon, 1974-2005)

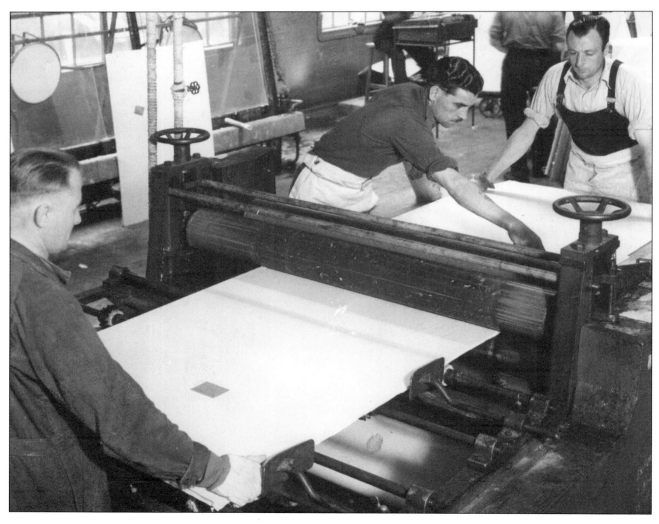

Sizing and cutting plasterboard.

Nylon Works

In 1967 I started at Nylon Works on the South Site. There was a huge turnover on that South Site. But some of the jobs were in quite horrendous sort of heat, heavy work, dusty, so I was very fortunate. I started with a pal of mine and he went to one end of the factory and I went to the other and we both went onto panel jobs which were quite cushy really compared to some of the other jobs. I started

They put me on the Nylon Works. We had what they call a bandcasting. The nylon came out of a big valve which was a metre wide. Like a ribbon. It went on to a stainless steel thing which was about thirty feet long. It revolved. And to cool this down there was water spraying all over the place. Then it went into dips and then it went into a chopper that chopped it all up. You had to move these casts, big machines by hand from one autoclave to the other. There were six autoclaves, a big container that mixes

Chopping cyanide in Cassel Works.

there as a holiday relief, the plant was called the KA Plant and that stood for ketone alcohol. It was a highly explosive plant. There was a panel man and there was another man worked another panel, a bit more complex panel and he was the leading hand. So it was a two-man job although it was quite a big plant. I was on there for about a year and then I moved onto a higher grade plant - they called that plant the HMD Plant and that stood for hexamethylenediamine.

(Maurice Benson, 1967-1999)

all the nylon. You got wet through. Then you got problems where you might get a jam and you would have to shut down quick and clear it. You had a certain time to get this autoclave empty before the next batch was running in behind it.

(Bill Henderson, 1966-1971)

My main job there was to oversee the extension of the Nylon Polymer Plant at Billingham. All the equipment was on site. All the materials were on site. Part of the steelwork was erected and I was there to see it through to the end. But in reality we never struck another bat on that all the time I was there. The writing must have already been on the wall for Nylon Billingham when I look back on one or two pep talks by directors and this type of thing. Looking at the state in general of the plant with the knowledge that you had, you then realised the writing was on the wall and they said, 'Well, we're just not going on with this extension.' The Polymer Plant was the limitation, was the bottleneck in the whole of the works. All the others were capable of more output but the Polymer Plant couldn't keep up with the output from the other parts of the plant. But they never did extend it. They never did any work on that.

(Tony Lynn, 1945-1989)

Nylon closed shortly after seventy-two because they'd built a new nylon plant at Ardeer. The old plant, the Billingham plant, was the oldest of the three plants. There was the Billingham plant and there was a plant at Wilton and the new plant at Ardeer signalled the end of the Billingham plant. Although the Billingham plant was the quality material it was the oldest plant and it was a plant that was maybe twenty-five years old, something like that. So Nylon closed round about seventy-two from what I remember

(Maurice Benson, 1967-1999)

Oil Works

I started two till ten in Oil Works as a process operator on circulation and conversion. And at that time there were still women working there, still they hadn't fully taken over by then. There were still women working on the system. They were still making petrol from coal. The crushing plant and everything was still there. Forty-six/forty-seven was a bad winter and we had a so-called coal shortage. Oil Works started to shut down bit by bit. They wanted to change Oil Works over to other processes from what they were already doing and to get government grants and one thing and another. They started to close these plants down, the old ones and shut them away. And ICI got money from different places to convert into carbonylation.

(Fred Moody, 1946-1982)

There was a lot of equipment and it was the old Petrol from Coal Plant built in 1936, so even in the nineteen-sixties it was antique technology. It was high pressure, it was running at about 3,000 pounds per square inch and it handled carbon monoxide and hydrogen, so if anything leaked you'd got flames out everywhere and then you've got all sorts of problems. It had been run right through the war making petrol and then it was changed to making chemicals for the plastics industry and also phenol which was sort of a general purpose chemical. Different technology, different materials, different processes, different materials in an old plant. It was all a bit difficult.

(Robert de Wardt, 1957-1981)

Oil Works naturally was very oily. It's alright as long as the oil stays in the pipes and the vessels but quite a lot of it comes out so things get oily and you're messing about and your hands get black, you can't get the colour off and all that kind of stuff. A funny point, it's really not important but I used to smoke at the time and at Oil Works you could only smoke in smoke huts. It was a fire hazard, you see. So you'd go into the smoke hut and you'd light up and all you could taste and smell was the oil. It was terrible, it wasn't very pleasant. But I worked at it as a youngster. I worked at it because I wanted to smoke. The other thing about Oil Works was that half of it was high pressure which is 250 atmospheres. That's a hell of a pressure so if you get a leak there it comes out like a rapier needle or, funnily enough, as a fire. So we worked on one plant, Four Stall it was called, it was making nonanol and we were working on this valve on the back. There was a big wall there, control room was one side and the back of it's where all the high-pressure vessels are. We were working on this valve quite a long time. We hadn't quite finished it so we went off for our lunch, we came back down after and we'd just walked in through the door to the control room. Just going out of the back door saying, 'We're off out there again,' to the process man and there's such a kerfuffle. The job we'd been working on had leaked, or near there there'd been a leak, a pipe, a big joint had fired. If we'd have been there we'd have had it. And that's a week back at work. So you don't think about it at the time, you think later, 'My God!'

(Ray Marriner, 1949-1985)

Ramsay MacDonald (left) at the opening of the Petrol Plant in 1936.

There was a phenol plant. It shut down while I was there but it was a beastly, horrible plant. Phenol is horrible stuff. If you get it on you it will burn you. It's very serious burns like acid burns and if that doesn't kill you it will stop your liver functioning so you die anyhow. I think if you got your hands covered you were as good as dead. It started off with a benzene compound. Stuff called monochlorobenzene and caustic soda. Now the benzene compound was inflammable. The caustic soda is corrosive and burns you again. This was pumped up to 3,000 pounds a square inch and put through tubes in a furnace. Big gas flames all round them and that produced the reaction which produced the phenol. Then it was taken out and separated down. But this stuff was so corrosive that steel pipes wouldn't stand up to it and anything that came into contact with the material had to be lined with nickel. So the pipes in the furnace were all lined with nickel and even then the nickel would give out at times. Then within a few hours the steel would go and all this lot sprayed out inside the furnace and you got flames going up the stack. And it got to the point they just put steam jets inside there so if the whole lot went off again you just pulled a lever and filled it with steam and that doused the flames. But if anybody went near the equipment and had to do any work, because of the risk of leaks, they had to be fully kitted out in PVC suits, helmets, complete cover over the head and that sort of thing. Even then there was one man who was standing up on some of the equipment there fully kitted and a leak did come and he did get sprayed all over his gear and I think the control room people saw what happened and said, 'Don't move, stay there.' They just put hoses on him to completely wash him down.

(Robert de Wardt, 1957-1981)

The butanols went down to the Paints Division at Slough. Some of the acetones were going to Ponds, the face cream people and phenols used to go to into making laminates and Formica and things like that. Plasticizers, of course, were used in the plastics industry. You know all your cables have got plasticizers in them to make them flexible.

(George McGee, 1951-1985)

They used to have three petrol grades - they had two-star, three-star and four-star. We used to make the grades of petrol and decide which bits were going into which. It's like a big cooking pot. We used to blend the petrol, store it and then send it out under fairly rigorous conditions. Because it's got a British Standard you had to keep to. There were also the safety aspects. I had probably sixty road tankers a day coming into the place and rail dispatches across to Manchester and occasional ship dispatches. But I used to do all the rail and road. That was the last job I had with ICI.

(George McGee, 1951-1985)

Products Works

I went back into Products Works. That's where they made fertilizers and the nitric acid and sulphuric acid. I moved around there quite a bit and did various jobs.

(Jim Steedman, 1946-1987)

Packing fertilizer, Nitro-Chalk. It came through above us; you put these thick paper sacks on and clamped them on. Then it came down and filled it and then you released it with a lever. Then it went down the line on a conveyor belt. There were two of us doing that side by side so you had to work your sacks in between each other so they don't both fall together. Anyway, there was a man folding the tops and then they went through a sewing machine and the girls sewed them up. Then straight down, they dropped through the floor and there was a loader there, one of the men, and he put it straight onto a lorry.

(Margaret Hopper, 1957-1961)

Prior to its closure in the early nineties, the CCF Plant was in the condition a six-foot snowstorm would have left it with the amount of dust and product residue. All the steelwork was rusty. A dust mask had to be worn on entering the building and goggles had to be worn for eye protection. Walk in one end of the plant in a black suit leave the plant in a white one.

(Barry Dunnill, 1956-1994)

Nitrates Avenue in the 1950s showing the Process Offices and the extensive gas and steam pipe bridges linking all the plants on the site.

Loading bagged fertilizer into rail wagons.

Hand sewing a urea bag.

Workers with protective masks sewing the tops of CCF bags in the late 1950s.

'I was better for it' Training and personal development

The education and training of ICI's workforce was seen as vital to its success. The company committed early in its history to 'provide such educational and training facilities that employees at all levels have the opportunity for progress and development'. Most divisions, including Billingham, appointed an education officer in the Personnel Department to organise educational and training courses and ensure the continued development of the workforce.

New appointees at Billingham were quickly introduced to the work of the Education Department in induction schemes. Billingham was one of the first divisions to initiate a new starters' course, where new workers were instructed on the history, philosophy and organisation of the company.

The training of craft apprentices took place in the company's own Apprentice School. All the apprentices initially took an identical course to introduce them to workshop practices, safety and accident prevention before they were trained in their chosen craft. After about a year in the Training Centre they were moved to a variety of different works to expand their experience. In 1956 a new Apprentice School was built on what is now Belasis Avenue, opposite North Gate, expanding the maximum number of apprentices who could be trained at any one time from about 75 to 200. A total of 15 trades could now be given initial training in the School, whereas in the previous Centre trades like joinery, sheet metal work and welding had to be taught on the job.

A Secretarial Training School was also opened at Billingham in the 1950s. This enabled the company to provide in-house commercial training rather than relying on external courses in local colleges. ICI claimed that the women could learn more about the company and the way they would be expected to work by receiving their training in the school.

In 1957 the first training course for process operators was established. Until this new development process workers learnt on the job from their workmates and supervisors. The course was designed to teach the principles behind the basic plant processes and the equipment operators would be likely to use. It was only intended to provide an introduction for new starters and most of the training still would be provided on each plant.

Craftsmen or process workers who were promoted to a supervisory role attended a training course at Norton House at Hardwick. The syllabus of the course included personnel management, labour policy, works' rules and accident prevention. Other classes were taught at this location including courses for employees in the Commercial Department and work study training.

For graduate staff, training was also organised to develop their technical and managerial skills. For instance, a staff course for plant managers developed their knowledge of plant activities and also the principles of good man management. There were specific courses organised for senior staff to improve skills such as public speaking and chairing meetings. As well as local initiatives, a central staff Training Centre at Kingston upon Thames provided a wide variety of centrally organised courses.

Whilst a great deal of training took place on site, many employees were encouraged to further their education at local colleges and universities. The company paid tuition fees and travelling expenses. Local technical colleges helped thousands of employees to gain relevant qualifications and Constantine College in Middlesbrough, which subsequently became Teesside Polytechnic and then University of Teesside, provided higher-level qualifications for suitable employees. ICI also provided scholarships for children of employees to study at university.

The extracts in this chapter reflect the wide variety of educational and training opportunities provided at Billingham.

Apprenticeships

I was taken on as an apprentice fitter. I can't recall how I was interviewed or how I was selected but like all apprentice fitters in those days, you started off by going into the main machine shop and doing the various things. I can remember standing on a box to reach the vice to do hammer and chisel routines, covered with bruises. I recall we used to work twelve-hour shifts. I presume it was when we became eighteen we did twelve hours. We used to work quite long hours. We used to work Saturday mornings in those days. It used to be a five and a half day week. I did the normal things. I went round the machine shop, I did some turning. I was more a fitter/turner than fitter. I did quite a bit of time in the valve shop. Then I worked on the Ammonia Plant and then I had a period down the anhydrite mine which was very interesting.

(Stan Buglass, 1937-1980)

We started an innovation with graduate apprentice training when they came from universities and did about a three-week course

Apprentice training.

The Engineering Training Centre on Belasis Avenue.

if I remember rightly. Practical training and I ran those. I was surprised because I had to get my hands dirty again by actually doing some filing and chiselling and things like that. But that was quite good. In fact, I've got a tankard at home which they gave me for that. Then we started doing graduate courses but that started when we go the new school. That was quite an innovation as well. I remember we taught them German at the same time. I don't know why we did this but we certainly had it. We were quite busy here. We also started doing technical apprenticeships as well.

(Stan Buglass, 1937-1980)

The apprenticeship started in forty-nine and we went into a little training centre which had been during the war a gunmetal shop where they used to make gun barrels. So it was a nice self-contained little place and we went into the fitting bay first and we were given instruction and practice in filing and drilling and chiselling, all the manual skills, all the hand skills. Then you went into machine bay where you learnt to turn and use milling machines. I was an instrument artificer the whole time on different plants in the apprenticeship. You see the thing about instrumentation - it's a very wide ranging job anyway. You've got the jobs ranging from very big heavy control valves on Oil Works where it was all high pressure - they were very heavy things, quite heavy work - to the finest of pneumatic detection, movement detection devices and electrical stuff. You ranged from very heavy stuff to extremely light stuff. So I think it was a great job. To be quite honest, if it hadn't been for the fact that you really had to get promotion to a higher level to get the increased earnings, I would still be a plant tiffy.

(Ray Marriner, 1949-1985)

But I thought that there were many things that a chaplain could do and stimulate. Let me tell you what their response was first. They thought that they'd test me out in the Apprentice

Centre at Billingham. It was taking in about 150 apprentices a year and over the four years there was a substantial number in a very large centre and they thought that they should see how I got on with that. It was again a case of the clergy look after kids up here and do youth work so let's see how he goes on in there. I did all sorts of things with them in no time. I got them withdrawn from their training, their technical training. They were offering technical training, practical training and, of course, academic back-up at the colleges. I was saying, 'There's something for life skills that I would like to introduce them to.' About working together, learning about themselves, learning about each other, working in teams. I walked around in the works eventually but in the Apprentice Centre I was given freedom to go in at any time I wanted, to let people know I was there of course and then just to walk around as they were doing the training on their benches or whatever it was. They filed and

filed and filed for thousands of hours in order to be able to become fitters and turners and all the rest of it and, of course, they were learning how to use machines. But I just stood alongside them, chatted away to them, got them going, got all sorts of responses.

(Bill Wright, 1959-1992)

Secretarial School

I trained as a shorthand typist. It wasn't in a typing pool as such. I was actually in the Training School. They had their own Training School. So we were trained there for about eight months and we learnt the whole history of ICI while we were there. We were taken round different areas of ICI, Billingham. Just so that we could get a general idea of what the whole thing was about before we were even allowed to go out into the factory to work. I found it quite amusing when we first started learning to type. The teacher brought a

Apprentice training.

metronome out. I couldn't understand why this metronome was there and then after that she started playing music and, of course, it was to get us into a regular rhythm so that we could keep a decent speed up.

(Gwen Mountain, 1956-1960)

The Secretarial School was a modern building right next to the Apprentice Training School which was a bit of nirvana as well. We went in there and it was quite intensive. You were there all day and all day you worked. I went to be trained as an audio typist and all day you were practising, practising and then you'd have your tea breaks and your lunch breaks and at lunchtime you'd walk up to the canteen. You got a little blue card when you got there, when you were under eighteen, which entitled you to a very cheap meal in a great canteen. The food was wonderful. I think it was one and tuppence you paid with your little blue card and you got a meal. I used to remember at break times you had a proper tea lady with a green uniform bringing your morning coffee and afternoon tea and little cakes and biscuits. Things you took for granted but now you'd think was really classy and then was just the norm.

(Linda Flintoff, 1964-1976)

Local college courses

I was told they would give day release in order that I could continue with my studies and that's what I did. I went to what was then Constantine Technical College. It was a remarkable college since it was sponsored by the Constantine family and it was quite unique in its day. It was particularly orientated round the type of studies I was interested in so I benefited in many ways from not only working on the subject I was interested in but also being supported by ICI in my further studies at a college.

(Alf Illingworth, 1952-1969)

You did a day release and a night school. We went to Nelson Terrace in Stockton for the day and then on a night we went to one which was further up the same road. It was a school during the day but we used it for night school on a night. Most of it was City and Guilds so it was practical and it was all about sheet-metal

work. Different metals, how they worked. How they heated up, what you needed to do with them and practical work – soldering, welding. The drawing was all development work which you used all the time at work. It would have taken you years to pick it up in doing the actual work.

(Mike Thompson, 1952-1990)

I started off in 1970 doing an ONC which was a day release equivalent to A-Level in physics, chemistry and maths. So that progressed my chemical knowledge mostly which was applicable to work and I did that for three years because really I bunked one year. You think it's a bit of a lark at first. I was a bit resentful because you were expected to go. It wasn't really an option, you were told to go because the company wanted you to get on and some of us treated it as a bit of lark. When you fail the exams the first time you get a right dressing down. I got a right dressing down from Personnel and had to start again at the beginning.

(Eric Collins, 1970-1976)

The day release went right through the apprenticeship. It was a full day, nine in the morning till about twenty to eight and then we were away. If you didn't go there was a warning system of verbal warnings and written warnings leading to dismissal. So it was very, very well policed.

(David Sutheran, 1978-1982)

I had a chief at that time who took an interest in his staff at their annual assessments and I said, 'What do you think would be a good thing for me to do at evening classes this year?' He said, 'Learn German. Everybody who has a good education should know French but anyone interested in chemistry should also know German.' So I made it my business to go to evening classes at what was then Middlesbrough High School and took French and German together. I used to cycle from Eaglescliffe to Middlesbrough about four nights a week after work, cycle home from work, from Billingham to Eaglescliffe and then another six miles or so to Middlesbrough after that. I enjoyed my German lessons so much that eventually someone suggested to me when I was saying I felt I wanted to go to university but I didn't see how I could possibly afford it and someone said why don't you study in Germany. This was a German lady who had been born in Germany. I was interested and my own boss had taken his doctorate degree in Frankfurt and I asked him about it and he said, 'Yes, of course, why not. If you get launched into a doctorate degree course there you just simply can't fail, you just go on until you're turned out at the other end as a doctor.' So I thought that sounded right. I didn't know how I was going to afford it but at that time people used to put a contribution every week into the Savings Bank. So I had a little nest egg there.

(Kenneth Warne, 1922-1968)

On the job training

The first thing I did when I started working was sat in a corner of the lab on a stool with the book of safety regulations; and until I could quote chapter and verse I wasn't allowed to stir except to make a cup of tea or something. That was it. I sat for about three days just learning everything in this book until you knew which way and every way. Then the first thing they said was, 'What do you know about reflecting furnaces?' I said, 'Not a lot,' and they said, 'well, you will do by the time you've made one and there's the drawings, get to work.' So we set to work to make this thing and almost got it finished and they changed their mind, they weren't going to do it that way any more and so I never actually saw my reflecting furnace in use.

(Allan Wilderspin, 1953-1955)

We had a three-month training period, or more maybe. I was about twenty-two; we were expected to stay there till we were sixty-two, that's forty years. What's six months in forty years, you know, for proper training? And you know that Billingham is a big place. We did a work's tour lasting at least four weeks where we went all around different bits of the works. We saw every plant, we saw everything, we saw everybody, we really knew how that place worked and ticked. At the time a group of us were an experiment, the arts graduate in industry. I think the jury's still out as to whether it failed or succeeded. First of all, we

were all put into a room and they said, 'Right, good.' It was still like being in the Air Force, 'Good show,' and he'd probably been in the Air Force too. He said, 'Now, any of you got blues?' Several people put their hands up. 'Right,' he said, 'you'll be in Labour Department, the chaps who can play sport. And now the rest of you, I suppose you were rather boring and got good degrees?' 'Oh, yes, yes, we've got good degrees.' 'Right,' he said, 'you'll go into Sales Control,' which was what marketing was then called. All this dates from the war when sales had to be controlled and allocated and everything. 'You'll go into Sales Control. They need a bit of brains there, I'm told.'

(Julian Phillips, 1956-1985)

When I first started there, it was an eye opener. I didn't think of ICI as having places like drum making plants. I thought ICI was all chemicals. The diameter was fourteen inches to twenty-two inches which were what we called the oil drum, the twenty-two inch. It wasn't the same as an oil drum but it was the same type as an oil drum but they were open topped mainly.

Drumming cyanide pellets on Cassel Works.

What we called open top drums. They didn't have a seal on like an oil drum. They had a lid and a fastener but there was none sealed, apart from the ones we sent over to Ammonia. They had a sealed top. They showed you what to do. How to do it safely and you gradually built yourself up through into speed. If you can imagine, if you just go onto a piece of machinery and you've just learnt it you can't do the speed of the production line, so the production would suffer so you had to quickly pick it up. In those days you were on bonuses, you had to make a bonus. So if you were in the middle of a line and you were holding everybody up, everybody was losing bonus so they would say to you, 'Pick it up, pal.'

(Bill Smith, 1964-1998)

Company training courses

In the first ten years of my time with ICI, particularly when I was this side of thirty-five, I had no end of training. If there's one thing that ICI did very well, that was training its young managers, particularly those with good potential. If they could see somebody's got potential then they'd put a huge amount of training their way. Every year I must have gone on one or two major training experiences, whether they were a course or whatever. All of that stands me in great stead now. I still do things that people think is rocket science but I was taught to do it when I was thirty. An awful lot of organisations don't make that investment and people don't develop anything like as well as we were trained. I have to say I was very, very well trained by the company and, you know, I was better for it. But I think I still am a lot better for it. I feel that I've experienced more things because of the training and development activities that I received than I would have done in most organisations. It was terrific, no question about it.

(Keith Farmery, 1970-2000)

In those early days most of that training was heavily focused at Norton Hardwick and very little else of it was being done locally. I think later on in Engineering Works and in Ammonia Works, they were beginning to mount local training. Team building exercises with the new processes coming on line and that kind of thing.

(Tony Brennan, 1955-1985)

Hartburn House, the home of many training courses.

One of the things that I did as a plant manager was develop a business appreciation course for all staff. So I, not on my own but with one or two others, developed the course and then we actually conducted it. So the process operators, the fitters, the riggers, whatever, along with their supervisors, all went on that course without exception and we led it. Other courses were generated by external organisations and people went on that as well.

(Keith Farmery, 1970-2000)

But I had, also, to be 'Curried'. Now at the time ICI had a bonus scheme which was based on work study so every young engineer and manager had to go to London to the company training establishment there to be trained in work study and method study and the guru was R M Currie. So it was known as being 'Curried'.

(Edward George, 1958-1988)

Secondment to university

Then the company sent me and three other people to Loughborough College. Before it was Loughborough University it was Loughborough College of Technology and they sent four of us to Loughborough to do the last year of a degree course because they were sort of sussing Loughborough out as a possible venue for some of their student apprenticeships. 'We'll send this lot and we'll get their views on what they thought of the place as well as give them a bit of further education.' I was married then. I was twenty-seven I think when I went there and I was married and we had no children but we had just moved into a house in Billingham so I only got home every three weeks. But I enjoyed the time there.

(Jim Steedman, 1946-1987)

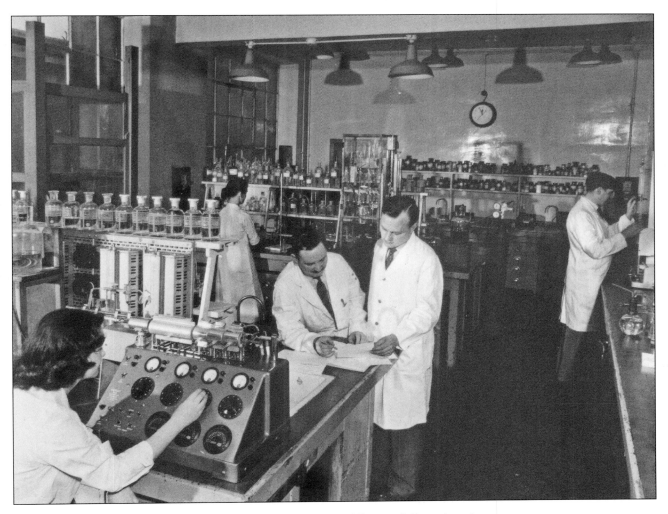

Organic Chemicals Section of Research Department.

Chapter 5

'They were quite strict'
Conduct and discipline

When employees began work they were presented with a Rule Book. It was an essential handbook informing workers 'what to do and what not to do' and ensured they worked in 'safety and harmony'. They were encouraged to read the book because 'ignorance of a rule cannot be accepted as an excuse for breaking it'.

The most significant rules related to safety, theft, timekeeping and acceptable conduct whilst on site. Any incident of misconduct had to be reported to a personnel officer before any action was taken to ensure uniform standards of treatment were maintained. Punishments varied from an informal warning to summary dismissal.

The next extracts demonstrate how the workforce reacted to such policies and more importantly provide valuable insights into the unwritten rules of everyday conduct which contribute so much to the culture of any organisation.

Standards of conduct

I was a messenger boy and I worked in the post room under an ex-army sergeant who used to keep us ruled with a rod of iron. Our trousers had to be pressed on a morning. Our fingernails were examined and we went on our daily rounds.

(Don Miller, 1943-1971)

But he was also the man who kept his eye on the general conduct and discipline of the place. Particularly for young men and women in the lab he used to keep a fatherly eye on what you were doing and how you were doing things. There were occasions when people started assembling and having a good natter and he

used to come along and say, 'I think you've spent far too long chewing that piece of cud. You'd better move on and get on with some work.' He was there to do a job and you respected him for it and you just had that degree of discipline anyway. But ICI also had that opportunity to make sure it was also observed in your working environment as well. I can never remember anyone having a row or a shouting match.

(Alf Illingworth, 1952-1969)

We just wore our normal clothes but they were very, very particular about you wearing stockings. You weren't allowed to wear trousers, you had to wear a skirt and they didn't like you to overdress. I can remember when I was there, one young lady came in and I think she was one of the messenger girls. She had been out the previous night and she came in the next morning in this off-the-shoulder dress, lots of jewellery round her neck and she was sent home.

(Patricia Whyman, 1957-1964)

There was a set of rules and there was a pattern to follow, if you like. There was nothing left to your own imagination.

(June Challenger, 1949-1950; 1969-1985)

Disciplinary offences

There were more people there than what was outside in Billingham. It was a marvellous place and especially at half past four at night when you used to stand at the West Gate. They used to stand there about eight deep on bikes waiting to get out. They daren't go until that buzzer went and sometimes there was the labour officer there. If he saw you there three minutes before half past four he used to take your name and number.

(Tom Boumphey, 1944-1987)

Workers leaving the Billingham Site at Chilton Avenue.

I joined ICI in fifty-one. It wasn't too bad because don't forget I'd done two years National Service so I was conditioned. Because ICI was a very, what I would call, regimental type of organisation, you had this strict hierarchy. From the works manager downwards you had a hierarchy which wasn't completely different from the way the Air Force operated. So I was conditioned by the time I got to ICI to expect levels of discipline which ICI insisted upon. The big thing about ICI was your timekeeping had to be spot on. We used to get five minutes a week allowed and you could use a minute a day or any proportion - two minutes and three, or anything like that or you could use it in one five minute block. But if you used your five minutes that was it, you know, you're dead. You got quarter houred. Then also it went against you when staff grade came up and staff grade was the marvellous thing. If you got staff grade in ICI you were walking on cloud nine.

(George McGee, 1951-1985)

I got into a bit of trouble for my timekeeping. First of all, you see the local supervisor and he'll say, 'Buck your ideas up,' and then the next was that you see a junior manager and he explains, gets all your history out, the books, time-keeping records which is supposed to be all black. I saw all those and then the last one I saw was the works engineer. I'm getting in serious trouble now. Anyway, I went to see him in his office and he was sat there. He used to smoke a pipe and he was lighting this and his dog was laid down. And he said to me, 'What do you think about this?' And I thought, 'It's alright, what's the matter with it?' 'You see all these red things. That's when you were late. What's the problem?' So I said, 'Well, I can only get one bus,' and he said to me, 'the policy is that you should get up in time to walk to work, never mind get a bus. You're going to have to buck your ideas up, you know.' I'd been there a few years then. But that didn't save you. He said, 'You'd better find another method of transport or make sure you get that bus.' So I being stupid, I said, 'Why would that be?' He said, 'Well, if I see you again you'll be sacked.' That really did take me by surprise because up till then it'd been all easy, you see. So anyhow I went back to the cabin and, of course, all the lads knew I'd been up to see him and they all said, 'What did he say?' I said, 'Well, I'll have to pull my ideas up or I'm going to get the sack.' 'Oh,' they said, 'well look, you get a bike and come by bike. In case you are late we'll clock your card but make sure you get here.' So I got a bike.

(Dennis Carroll, 1952-1979)

You had proper tea breaks and that was quite organised. We also had to sign in and sign out. We didn't clock in, we signed in and they were quite strict with time because a line was drawn across and if you came in after that line was drawn across you lose quarter of an hour or whatever. You would lose quarter of an hour's pay for every five minutes or so that you were late. It was an incentive to get there on time. If you had a genuine excuse, if you had been to the doctor's or something like that or you had to come by bus and the bus had been held up in traffic, then yes, they would ignore it. But usually it was a case of, 'You know what time you're to be here. You're late. I am sorry we're going to have to quarter you.'

(Gwen Mountain, 1956-1960)

Gross misconduct

I was sat in the office and there was a bloke knocked on the door, 'Ray, so-and-so has gone missing.' So I said, 'Well, have you checked everywhere?' 'Yes, I've been down there to look around.' 'Aye,' I said, 'I'll come down and have a walk around.' So I walked down, we looked around and we were looking around the control room. We went up the stairs at one end. I said, 'What's in there?' The bloke said, 'Oh, that's just steam supply system.' So I opened the door. Here's this fella laid on the floor with overalls and things on and he's sleeping. So I'm kind of nudging him and, 'Up you get and get back to the shop straightaway now.' So got him back there and I said, 'Do you realise you're still at work? It's important that people should know where you are. We've had

a site hazard out on you looking for you and unless you've got a damn good excuse I'm going to dismiss you,' because he already had a poor record. He had other things on his file. And he said, 'Well, I'm working as a bouncer in a nightclub and I'm not getting to bed till early morning.' 'Oh,' I said, 'well, try and get yourself a full-time job there then. You just go up and see Personnel Department on Friday, they'll give you your papers and you're away, alright?' And that was it. But I thought about it later and I thought, 'Now why was it I was able to go and find him when they weren't?' They were just as astute as me looking in places. I think the lads in his squad had set him up because he was asleep. Probably doing it every day. They were getting sick of it.

(Ray Marriner, 1949-1985)

There was a guy who was going on holiday and decided that he'd like to do some fishing on his holiday so he went to a department store in Hartlepool and walked out with an armful of fishing gear that he didn't pay for. He was pursued by the security of the store in question. Jumped in his car and drove off but the security man got his number plate. The civil police visited him at his home and in the process of interviewing him had a look round and contacted ICI to say, 'We think you'd better come and have a look in this guy's garage.' So his manager and some of the Works Police went out and found his garage was stocked to the rafters with equipment that he had no authorisation to have in his possession, including a welding set, two cylinders, the trolley, the torches, the cables, everything. It would have taken a trailer to get it home. He had a block and tackle and chain with a hoist in his garage and all sorts of things. Now okay, that's an unfortunate incident. From a Personnel point of view the works manager comes to see me and says, 'What do we do?' And I said to him, 'He's suspended on full pay as of today pending the outcome of a civil prosecution with regard to the shoplifting theft. We'll wait to see what happens about that but then we will have to consider including charges for unlawful possession of company property.' The works manager in that case was arguing, 'What about the guy's family and so forth and so on, if we're going to do this we've got to do that.' I remember having to take, on one of the very few occasions, a very hard line with the works manager and saying to him, 'Sorry, you are not responsible for the welfare of that man's wife and children. The responsibility for the wife and children's welfare rests first and foremost with the man who's guilty of a crime.' When he eventually was found guilty by the courts for the civil offence we then discharged him for gross misconduct in respect to the ICI stuff. There was a nice little corollary that went on during that. His supervisor actually wrote to the works manager to say, 'This guy's been a very loyal servant to this company and has saved this company hundreds of thousands of pounds in the process of his work over the years. He's one of my best men and I hope you'll be able to treat him with the due amount of leniency.' The works manager brought that letter to me and I said, 'Well, I think there's two things that you need to do. One is to consign that to the dustbin, and the second thing is to interview that supervisor and ask that supervisor how come that bloke walked out of this establishment with all that gear and you, as his supervisor, didn't even know about it, or claim not to know about it?' Looking back on it there's a very fine line between managing from a human point of view and the concern that was the first instinctive reaction of the works manager for the welfare of the family. And because that was his first instinctive reaction there was a need, as I saw it at the time, to balance that with saying, 'Just a minute. This is a business.'

(Tony Brennan, 1955-1985)

So by sixty-two I'm very conscious of the safety aspect and so I used to go into the plant at night times and at weekends when the people on the plant didn't know I was coming. One infamous shop steward was sitting in the centre of the Oxygen Plant rolling his own cigarettes and I had him. I wanted to sack him on the spot but I was told that I couldn't do that and so I had the man in to tell him what I thought about him, knowing full well that I couldn't sack him but I could suspend him. He was one of the best actors I've ever met in my life because the tears rolled down his cheeks,

he said what his wife would do to him and he pleaded and begged me not to suspend him. Anyway, I had the pleasure of suspending him for three days. I went to a safety symposium at Harrogate a few weeks later and the secretary of that man's union was one of the speakers at the symposium. I felt somewhat aggrieved that this man hadn't been sacked and the secretary of his union said that ICI were lily-livered, 'My members were put at risk, he should have been sacked.'

(Gill Bowness, 1956-1991)

There was a system in place, they just didn't come and sack you or anything. You were warned. You had a verbal warning. You had a written warning and if you didn't heed them they would take real drastic action on you. I've seen a lad get sacked one day. He got called over to the office and I said, 'What's happening?' This is in Cassel Works. He was a fitter, a young fitter. And he says, 'I'm going home, I've been sacked.' But you see he'd been warned and warned and warned. He just didn't go in that day and get sacked. The shop steward told me, he said, 'There's nothing I could do about it, he'd been warned.' So he'd been warned and better warned. He was just a bad timekeeper, persistently bad timekeeper which they were very strict on. That was the main thing they were sticklers on was timekeeping. You know you just didn't get sacked in ICI. You just didn't. You know they had procedures and that would be the last they wanted to do.

(Ronald Dowd, 1970-1990)

Rule Book

In the eighties at Billingham we developed a completely new Works Rule Book. Now the Works Rule Book went back into the mists of history. And, of course, it was a key document if you were looking at aberrations of behaviour and so on. But it was decided that it didn't really fit for the time and the problem is, when you have to carry the trade unions with you, they're not exactly keen to bring out rules that will hang some of their members. But it had to be done and it was accepted that it was important that it was updated so we did a complete new Works Rule Book at Billingham

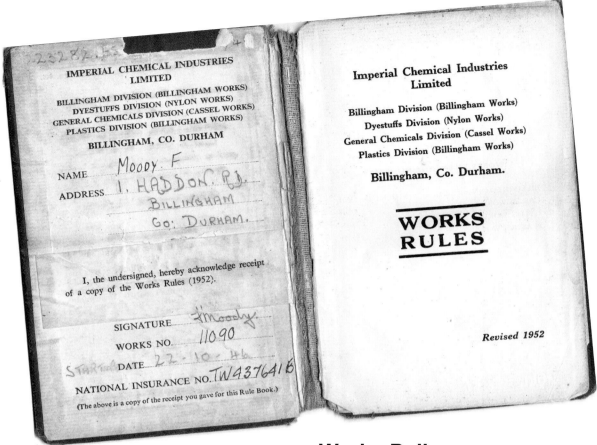

Rule Book.

which I led. I was effectively the project leader. It took about eighteen months to two years and everyone, I think, did their bit and there was so much toing and froing and getting into discussion and negotiation and arguing. And, of course, it meant that you had to persuade people that however defensive they wanted to be that was just essential in a modern rule book. So eventually we got through and the company seemed quite pleased that that was eventually achieved.

(Robin Cook, 1961-1993)

We carried the Green Book, the Rule Book. The Rule Books, in theory, were our ID. We had a card there like that. But we had to carry the Works Rule Book in case you were challenged by the safety man - the 'green hats'.

(David Sutheran, 1978-1982)

Works Police

The foreman came round and said they wanted people to go on patrols. You know they were starting up a new system, a patrol system, he said, 'Do you fancy it?' I said, 'Yes,' because I liked moving around. I wasn't too keen on just being sat in one place all the time. I was used to being out and about. So I put in for patrols and when I had been on patrols for a year they said, 'Well, do you fancy Works Police?' I said, 'Yes.' So they put my name in for that and I was selected.

(Tom Boumphey, 1944-1987)

They had Works Police. Initially there was a gateman and then they got the Works Police. Maybe they had a tip off, I don't know, but they would stop people. There would be random stops. But again you could borrow tools. If you wanted to borrow a set of particular tools for a job you were doing at home, you got your little chitty. It would say that you are authorised to borrow this. You could do it. So if you didn't get a little chitty, well, you're stealing.

(Jim Steedman, 1946-1987)

'It was paramount'
Safety at work

The nature of the chemical industry forces any company to take the issue of safety seriously. ICI had clear lines of responsibility for safety, reaching from company director level down to the individual employee. Safety matters were discussed regularly at company, division, works and plant level.

As part of the induction process, new employees were introduced to company safety policies and reminded of their own responsibility to maintain a safe environment. Whilst it was the responsibility of the management to provide appropriate conditions, equipment, training and supervision, employees had an important role to play in accident prevention. Company safety policy stressed that, 'safety should not take second place to production. All necessary steps to prevent accidents take precedence over all other activity. It is the duty of every employee of the company to do everything practicable to prevent injury to himself and others'.

There were regular safety drives in the factories and safety competitions were organised on a local and national basis. For instance, an inter-works safety competition began in 1947 offering money, trophies and gift prizes for improved safety figures. Employees were encouraged to train as first-aiders and first-aid competitions were a regular feature of life in the works. Some workers also became volunteer fire-fighters and the company paid an extra allowance to them for taking on this important role.

The importance of safety was publicised regularly. Posters and messages were displayed in prominent locations. Safety handbooks, calendars, leaflets and stickers emphasizing the importance of personal contribution to safety were published frequently and circulated amongst staff. The Billingham Post, the local company newspaper, was also used to disseminate the safety message. There were regular news reports of employees who had escaped injury by wearing their protective clothing. Those avoiding accidents by using safety protective goggles could become members of the Golden Eye Club and similarly those wearing safety footwear became part of the Golden Shoe Club. The Post also highlighted groups of workers receiving safety bonus awards for avoiding lost-time accidents for long periods.

Training and equipment were provided for specific hazards such as gas leakages. Breathing apparatus was on hand and relevant employees were trained in its use. Those working in areas where there were dangerous chemicals were encouraged to find out where respirators, eye wash bottles, water tubs and sprays were situated before starting a job.

The company kept detailed records of accidents and used these to improve their safety procedures. All workers were encouraged to report incidents however minor. The records show that the most common form of accident was falls and plant tidiness campaigns were used to help reduce the number of people suffering this type of accident. There were unfortunately still some serious and even fatal incidents on occasions. For example, three men were killed and 13 injured by an explosion in the Oil Gasification Plant in 1959.

Many of the older workers who were interviewed felt that safety was not so much of a priority in the early years of their employment but certainly ICI records show that by the 1950s, the company was constantly trying to motivate their employees to consider safety one of the highest priorities. How workers responded to this can be seen in the following extracts.

Views about safety at ICI

There were leaks in ammonia plants where your eyes were absolutely streaming. You know problems like this, people just took it in their stride and resolved the danger. They didn't say, 'I'm sorry I can't do that for the simple reason in ten years time I'll drop down dead or cancer'll hit me.' I can't remember people worried about that sort of thing.

(Mansell Shotton, 1942-1984)

I'm amazed when you think back, the security systems now in place as compared to then. I'm amazed the whole of Teesside didn't blow up. We used to walk around in asbestos, and look at the big scandals now about asbestos. We used to roll about in it. We used to do things with no safety precautions at all.

(Ginger Hawthorne, 1953-1964)

I couldn't fault ICI because I think if there was an accident in there it was unfortunate. I think that they did everything. I thought it was one of the safest places I ever worked even though it was the most hazardous. And I felt safe in there.

(Barry Dunnill, 1956-1994)

Generally speaking a lot of the accidents I came across were what I call domestic accidents. Cuts, tripping over something. One of the canteen attendants who insisted on wearing open toed sandals got a splinter in her big toe. Eventually the rules changed where you could say, 'That's no good, you've got to wear proper shoes.' And the same thing with safety helmets, you see. They weren't compulsory when I joined. There was a great fuss about how you persuade people to wear safety helmets. Well, fortunately we had a photograph of a chap wearing one with a spike sticking in the top and his life had been saved. That got everyone wearing one. The same problem with goggles. The riggers used to say, 'You can't wear a safety helmet and be a rigger, it doesn't work.' You had to do quite a bit of education. Noise was another one that was a developing problem and, of course, asbestos was because some of the things weren't known about. Noise wasn't appreciated and then it came in and then we had to be particularly careful about that.

(Edward George, 1958-1988)

Families on a works open day viewing protective equipment.

Equipment and clothing

The Sodium Plant, it was a killer. Conditions, the material they worked with. My father had to wear what they called fustian cloth and the only way I can describe it as flannel about that thick, about a quarter of an inch thick, his trousers and his coat and everything he had to be dressed like this. Then he had to have a hood over his face and goggles and gloves. They made sodium and the heat was terrible.

(Bob Tucker, 1937-1949)

The best thing I ever remember and someone brought this out, just out of the blue - all the mirrors in the factory had across the top, 'this man is responsible for your safety'.

(Mike Thompson, 1952-1990)

You couldn't go on any job without a work permit written out and signed. So any job had to be assessed. All the safety precautions had to be taken and then you had to be given this work permit. You had to read it or have it read to you and you had to sign it and whatever equipment you required, if they said you will

Workers with protective clothing in the sodium cell room, Cassel Works.

We had lads who would go on the grindstone. They'd look round to see if anyone was there. I said, 'What are you looking for?' 'Well, I am looking to see if the gaffer is coming, I want to grind this off.' I said, 'Well, get your goggles on.' Like he didn't need them on if he wasn't there. I said, 'He's not going to lose his eye.' Then they even had goggles on the side of the machine in boxes and they still would do things without using them. But it didn't take long for people to realise that it was for your benefit.

need a pair of plastic gloves and boots, you will need goggles, you will need a gas mask. Things like helmets and safety boots were compulsory and they would have it all listed, what equipment you had to have and you didn't go into that area to start a job unless you had the right equipment.

(Dave Peacock, 1960-1972)

They were on the ball, ICI with safety, weren't they? Especially the wearing of helmets,

Children trying on safety equipment at an open day.

goggles, earmuffs which I know people played hell at the time but when you look back when you get a bit older they were very beneficial to you, especially the earmuffs and hard hats and things like that.

(Ron Wilson, 1960-1989)

When I first went to Nylon, the noisiest, wettest plant on the Site, on the casting floor they suddenly brought out you had to wear helmets, full visors, earmuffs which you'd never worn before. So first thing you did was take it off. But then as soon as the gaffer was walking round, you'd rush to get your helmet back on again. But under those conditions, they were concerned about your hearing and your sight and, of course, you had to wear a hard hat all the time.

(Frank Curry, 1969-1985)

Billingham was a dangerous place, operating with toxic gases at high pressures and high temperatures so it needed strict rules and guidelines. Safety was paramount and it proved to be a safe place to work in, although there were always some accidents.

(Dennis Duggan, 1959-1998)

Ron Wilson pictured with hard hat.

Safety precautions

Safety sampling meant going round. They'd get trained observers to follow a set route through an area on a regular basis, like once a week, and note all the way round that route how many safety hazards they could identify.

(Tony Brennan, 1955-1985)

I think the attitude over the years started to change as the Health Service started to improve and started to have better facilities and where people weren't financially disadvantaged by this. So I think there was a gradual change over the period basically because the environment which the factories were set changed rather. I think gradually, the attitudes of the company said, 'Look, do we need to spend this amount of money on this and that? Should you be doing this?' More and more they went away from clinical medicine and the care of people to preventative medicine. So latterly we were more targeted

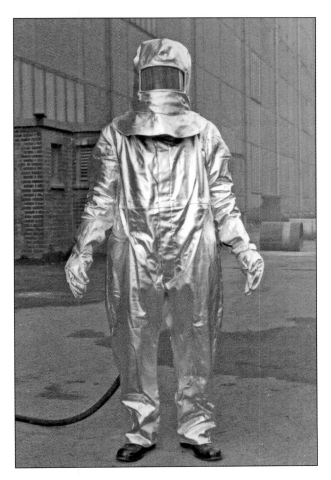

Worker wearing protective clothing.

towards early diagnosis of possible ill effects of chemicals and doing studies to really explore if certain diseases were being caused by chemicals which we were able to identify at an early age and correct it. Again, because of the national hysteria about chemicals, I spent a lot of time providing data for the Health and Safety Executive. Well, you think there's a problem with something like formaldehyde, somebody found it caused nasal cancer. But we were able to show you that people had been working with formaldehyde with us for fifty years and these were the statistics. We kept medical records of people. We also knew what they died of and so on and so forth. So obviously when they left us they were usually pensioned so that when they died the cause of death was recorded. So we knew that Mr Bloggs came in at age fifteen and died at seventy-eight of lung cancer or liver disease. So we could tell. We knew what the health experience was. This was shared with the unions and we worked closely with the unions. It was very seldom we had anybody, any groups of people, saying that they didn't want to work there or they were scared to work there. But they did feel that they were being cared for. You know that the trade unions had their medical advisors too. So essentially we tried to make sure that people were cared for on a day-to-day basis but also on a lifetime basis. That whatever materials they were handling they weren't going to absorb it or get enough to cause them any problems.

(David Bryson, 1962-1992)

We had to be de-matched when we went on site. We had to sign to say that we had no flammables, any lighters or matches.

(Maurice Benson, 1967-1999)

Safety training

There were minor accidents. People did get hurt but I don't remember any serious lasting injury. There were no deaths while I was there. The restrictions were good, you were trained, you got safety training every year. When anybody new came in one of the first things you were told was, this place is dangerous. There are hazards there because they do this, the heat, chemicals and in these circumstances you must wear this equipment, that equipment. Make sure you've got a clearance certificate before you even touch a job on the plant. All that kind of thing. The clearance certificate was just a matter of a process man saying to you, 'The job is safe for you to work on but the following hazards exist.' So once that had been signed over to you or your supervisor in those days, you would get your instructions to be told what to do on the job.

(Ray Marriner, 1949-1985)

We were taken down to this closed room. We were taught how to use - I think it was called a Salvus set which was an oxygen re-breather. Every now and again you had to open the valve at the bottom and squeeze this sort of bag in front of you, air-tight bag in front of you, to get rid of the CO_2 you were generating. But you just re-breathed everything until the bag got sort of fully inflated and you couldn't breathe out any more so you just had to release them.

Then we were taken into a room that was filled with ammonia and this is where the problems arose. It was a damp day. Our clothes were damp and we walked into the works and we came out and no one told us how bad this concentration was going to be and we came out into the damp, walked back up through the plant and into the lab. The clothes started to dry out with the heat of the lab. And everyone is coughing and spluttering with ammonia. Practically coughing their lungs inside out.

(Allan Wilderspin, 1953-1955)

Accidents

Dangers did, in fact, occur. The most notable one was that in a particular boiler situation the slurry, it was the spent fuel there, was dropped into a very, very deep trench where the water was travelling through to dispose of the ash, over a bridge and into a settling pit. In that settling pit the cranes dug out the slurry, separated it from the water which transported

Safety Award presentation, Ammonia Works.

it and took it away by lorry or disposed of it or gave it away somewhere - got shot of it there. Somebody was walking in there and they hadn't put the railings up and the man fell into this high-speed flow of water. I didn't see that happen but it went through and finally out into where there was a bridge. The man actually went through a pump, right through what they call an un-chokeable pump and it carried him up over a bridge and settled him out in the other side. When they found the body it was completely undamaged. It had been right through an un-chokeable pump. The inlet eye of the pump must have coincided with his presence there because it was a slow moving un-chokeable pump. He went up and down again. Things like that did, in fact, occur but they were unusual, very unusual.

(Mansell Shotton, 1942-1984)

I had shift riggers working all through the night and there were always two. I came in the morning and read the log and one of the riggers had been taken to hospital. It was during the night. I hadn't been told, hadn't been called out. So immediately I set about enquiries as to what had happened and he'd broken his wrist. So I said, 'Well, you know, we'll have to follow this up. Where's his mate?

I'll need to interview his mate.' 'Oh, well, he's gone home.' So I said, 'Well, I'll have to go and see him but I'll go to the hospital when I can and see the chap and see what happened.' Well, it turned out he had been on his own. So he said, 'Well, you know, so-and-so came in and he was drunk so we sent him home.' I said, 'Why didn't you ring me at home and I would have arranged somebody else to come out?' 'Oh, we didn't think it was necessary.' So further enquiries and discreet detective work, I found that this man had been regularly on night shifts not being fit to work and he'd either had to come in, stayed asleep in the loft all night, been covered, or he hadn't come in and they had clocked on for him. You know it was all a bit naughty and it had only shown up by accident which is often how things turn out.

(Tony Lynn, 1945-1989)

That particular morning we went to work and when I got there I could see the crowds of people and I thought, 'Well, there's something off here.' They said, 'Oh, there's been an explosion.' Anyway, I got to the mine and later on I got called. You see the central air station was looked after by the mine fitters and electricians. Anyway, they were putting water down the air lines to put the fire out. There was

Men working in the anhydrite mine.

a flame when I got down about fifteen foot high, just looked like a blow torch. We got a great hefty instrument sent down and it was for monitoring the methane so we had to see to this thing, wire it up. And also one of the Mines Inspectors wanted a fan running. There were hundred-inch fans also you see. They had to see to some pumps. Well, the only two men that were injured were the two men that were involved. They were burned. It was known that one of them had lit up. You couldn't smoke down the mine.

(Stanley Hawksfield, 1950-1978)

I remember him getting burnt. We were up a chimney one day and he got burnt on his neck. We thought it was rain coming down. It wasn't, it was sulphuric acid coming down. I made haste to get down but he got stuck and it burnt his neck.

(Harry Irvine, 1951-1973)

The fitter went up there with his breathing set on and took all the nuts off and the leading hand said, 'Well, we've got to have a look in, so let's get the door off quickly.' Rushed up, grabbed the door. Thought he had taken a deep breath before he got there and walked backwards and he hadn't. He took another breath and fell over with the door on top of him and to which we afterwards said, 'Well, serves you right, you shouldn't have done it.' He hadn't hurt himself but it was a lesson to him. That is the sort of thing that happens.

(Robert de Wardt, 1957-1981)

But we did have some serious fatal accidents where people died. We had serious ammonia leaks where people died. And, of course, we had people falling from time to time. I would think in my time at Billingham there were probably half a dozen fatalities due to accidents that had happened. Of course, they are very traumatic. We also, of course, occasionally had fatal accidents on the road with our tankers. One of the most difficult things for a personnel officer to do is to go to the house of the person to break the news.

(Robin Cook, 1961-1993)

We were in training in the pipe-fabrication shop. The platers' shop was alongside us across the road. One of the oxygen cylinders was knocked over. Now I don't know if you're familiar with oxygen and acetylene cylinders but they have a brass valve on the top and a dial to show you pressure. It caught the edge of one of the workbenches and it sheared off. I wasn't in there at the time, we were next door, but it sheared off on the edge of this workbench. It took the brass top off and it finished up acting like a torpedo. It was a fair sized long place about seventy feet high with a big overhead crane. It went from one end of the shop, missed everybody and went through the wall at the other end. It took off. There was just this hole in the wall. It took off and went through there.

(David Sutheran, 1978-1982)

Sodium cell room, Cassel Works.

Chapter 7

'Take care of the people' Industrial relations

In 1927 ICI employed about 33,000 people and at its peak in the early 1970s there were about 137,000 employees. The success of such a large enterprise depended to a large extent on securing the cooperation of its employees. The first chairman, Sir Alfred Mond, set the tone for future industrial relations policy by announcing he wanted to win the workers' loyalty by 'foreseeing reasonable demands and ....granting them even before they were asked.' As well as providing benefits such as reasonable pay and conditions, ICI set up Works Councils to maintain communication channels between the company and workforce. They consisted of equal numbers of management and elected workers' representatives and dealt with issues relating to the safety and well-being of employees. However, pay negotiations remained outside the remit of the council system.

The paternalistic philosophy of the company and its focus on gaining the loyalty of its workforce led to an ambivalent attitude to trade unions for blue-collar employees. Whilst ICI recognised unions in the period before the Second World War, membership was low and the company refused to enter closed-shop agreements. However, in 1947 ICI introduced new negotiating procedures and agreed to recommend that their workers joined a union. In response, the unions recognised and agreed to work with the Works Councils which they had previously opposed.

Pay and conditions at work were at the heart of unions' concerns. In the 1947 negotiations the unions tried to revise ICI's Staff Grade Scheme which they thought led to unnecessary divisions amongst blue-collar employees. Staff grade was introduced in 1928 and under this scheme hourly-paid payroll workers were eligible for promotion after they had worked for five years. They enjoyed enhanced pay and conditions including the right to a month's notice, payment for bank holidays and full pay for sickness absence. Some workers complained that promotion to this grade could be decided on the whim of managers and this could lead to a sense of injustice amongst workers. Distinctions between manual workers were not abolished until the late 1960s with the introduction of the Manpower Utilisation and Payment Structure (MUPS) and then the Weekly Staff Agreement (WSA). These productivity packages were designed to remove restrictive practices and increase job flexibility. The company could then reduce staffing levels if necessary and increase productivity and profitability levels, essential in the difficult operating period of the late 1960s and 1970s when it faced increasing global competition.

After the implementation of MUPS, process workers were allowed to do some jobs that had previously been carried out by trained craftsmen and equally craftsmen could be asked to do general process work. All manual workers were then paid on an eight-grade scale and were given a substantial pay rise. But the scheme was not popular with all workers, particularly craftsmen and was ultimately replaced by WSA. When this was implemented in 1969, WSA offered another increase in wages and closed-shop agreements for unions, reflecting changing company attitudes to their relationship with trade unions.

In 1970 a joint consultation system for weekly employees replaced the system of Works Councils and workers' representatives in the new structure were now shop stewards.

Joint management and employee committees were organised at the level of local works, site, division and company. Negotiations were conducted on issues such as health and safety, pensions and other potential areas of conflict but pay negotiations were still undertaken at a national level between the Central Personnel Department and national union officials.

Amongst white-collar workers, ICI tried to encourage joint consultation rather than wholesale unionisation. Until the 1970s ICI claimed unionisation would be unhelpful and that staff committees were a more useful system of representation. It is clear ICI still did not believe that the unions shared the same objectives and interests. However, in line with the experience of manual trade unions, support for white-collar unions was increasing.

ICI prided itself on its good industrial relations record and there was a low level of strike activity throughout its history: until 1986 there had never been a national ballot on strike action over pay. There had, however, been the occasional strike and this was also the case at Billingham.

The majority of the people we interviewed presented positive accounts of the way the company handled industrial relations and their own relationship with managers and work colleagues. It is clear many lamented the demise of the paternalistic style of management so apparent in the early life of the company. Some, however, were a little more ambivalent about their relationship with the unions as the following extracts show.

Consultative meetings

ICI accepted the unions. Nobody wanted them in those days. They were seen as obstacles in the way of progress, communists, people who wanted to destroy them and things like that. There was a sort of phobia about. But eventually the unions argued at senior level that these jobs should be done by representatives of the workers. The Works Councils were elected but not like shop stewards. They had to go and vote and like all voting you wouldn't get that many people going. They had different ones for each works. We had one in ours who was brilliant at pensions. People don't know about pensions, can't understand them, but this guy really concentrating on them was very good. Most of them just went along and they were seen to represent them but they didn't in that sense. They talked if they'd got complaints about the toilets or the canteens. The business that we were dealing with was the conditions and things like that wasn't their business. So it wasn't on their agenda. Eventually over a period of time, a long period of time, they came to accept it and therefore the union took over all that job.   (Dennis Carroll, 1952-1979)

The company introduced a new and modified staff committee system as a much more powerful, more structured, joint consultative organisation for monthly staff. It was clearly intended to stave off for as long as possible monthly staff unionisation. So they set up a whole lot of staff committees for each department and 'muggins' got nobbled as the representative of the training outfits. So I found myself sitting on a staff committee. We lectured and chatted and directed and raised hell. And not having had enough sense to keep my mouth shut I eventually found myself appointed as that committee's representative to the Division Standing Committee and went to its first meeting where one or two people who knew me from the training outfit recognised that here was a bloke that could shoot his mouth off and rabbit and rabbit and rabbit, so the process continued. But I was appointed as the first chairman of the Division Standing Committee just because I didn't keep my mouth shut often enough.
(Tony Brennan, 1955-1985)

Central Council at Scarborough, November 1961.

The company, I think, right from its start thought that it was appropriate, necessary for there to be a direct dialogue between the senior management of the company and of the divisions which are the major operating units within the company and key representatives. In the first instance they were not union representatives they were called Works Councillors. Later on the Works Council system was abolished as part of the reforms that brought the movement towards single status conditions of employment into the company. The Works Council system was replaced by Works Committees which had union representatives, shop stewards' representatives, ex-officio representatives on the Works Committees, then through Division Committees through to Central Committees which made provision for meeting at division and central level once or twice a year. Works Committees met every month with the works manager discussing business issues. Now for me, the Works Committee was great because I could show them the trading accounts all the time and we talked about dull things, about

what the competitors were doing and what could we do to address the issues. I personally found it very useful to work out what was going on in transport because I could talk to the representatives regularly. I could put things on the agenda. If it was a negotiation they were usually telling me what the agenda was. Here was a situation where I'd say, 'Hey chaps, you've got to listen. This is the state of the nation. This really is the state of the nation.' Some of my colleagues didn't seem to have the same opportunity.

(John Robinson, 1969-1989)

MUPS and WSA

MUPS, it was called and it promised to make everybody equal because, at that stage, in the paint shop I had seven grades to deal with. So there were seven rates of pay for different levels of painters. Of course, the sign-writer was on the top grade, he could do gold leaf and everything else. He could paint, he could go and paint handrails, he could do what you wanted him to do. Whereas down at the

Products Works Work Council of 1954 outside the front door of the Main Offices.

bottom end of the scale there was the person that you would only put on to paint handrails and only put the undercoat on. We wouldn't let him do the top coat even. So you were able to pay them by their ability to be able to do more jobs.

(Tony Lynn, 1945-1989)

There was a shortage of skilled labour and the industrial relations on the whole of Teesside were very difficult. Remember, inflation was picking up. In fact, this was the period when inflation was getting quite serious but people were demanding more money, tradesmen were demanding more money. They had refused to accept MUPS because they saw it again as something that would lead to the erosion of jobs and not sufficient reward so it was a bit of a hornets' nest.

(George McKinlay, 1957-1985)

Weekly Staff Agreement. It was when they were trying to get rid of some of the demarcations between unions and process workers. Simple things. They wanted process workers to be able to do very simple maintenance instead of

calling fitters in to do something like tightening a gland or anything that you needed a spanner to operate it. Simple things like that. Job descriptions for everybody had to be written and I was part of a team involved in preparing these job descriptions for getting the thing moving. There was a specific team involved in trying to get this organised and integrated into the ICI system. It wasn't just at Billingham, it was ICI-wide. So we had constant talks with union people and our own managers. The idea was that fitters wouldn't want mates and fitters would have to do simple jobs and that would mean downsizing.

(Jim Steedman, 1946-1987)

Relationship with unions

In the seventies and the eighties industrial relations was a major issue. It was a national issue and there were strikes all over the place. There were union forces working in the car industry, in the steel industry and the products sector and Lord knows where. The TUC had immense power and access to the Prime

Minister and all that kind of stuff and ICI was not immune from any of that. ICI, though, quite deliberately recognized the importance of good industrial relations. ICI had worked extremely hard at it. That was for me one of the characteristics of working for ICI. If you wanted to do some engineering then you did it very well, that was the expectation. If you wanted to do a job then you did that very well. And if you wanted to do industrial relations you did that very well. I remember when I was appointed to my first job there in the Methanol Plant my boss said, and this is an indication of the clarity of management, it's a big plant and it was full of energy so it was high hazard and with very expensive kit, so he said, 'Don't burn the place down, don't bust the big machine and don't have a strike. So take care of the process, take care of the hardware and take care of the people.' That was the remit I got, then he said, 'I'll see you next year.' That was very clear. The implication was that you had to do all those things very well and that applied to industrial relations.

(Keith Farmery, 1970-2000)

When I arrived at Billingham it was a very, very nice set-up commercially the company was in. They were the leading fertilizer manufacturer in the UK with a very, very weak number two who was beholden to them for buying quite a lot of the major feedstock, which was ammonia. I think ICI was a paternalistic company and if they had a free choice they'd probably preferred not to have trade unions there but they came to recognise that that was unrealistic. That wasn't going to happen. The unions were there so ICI decided that what it was going to do was to neutralise the unions as much as possible by giving them good facilities. That was double-edged in some respects. It also enabled ICI to ply the unions with information, business information and if you drip away at that often enough you would get over to people that you've got to make a profit and costs have got to be controlled and that sort of thing. I think there was also an element of cosying up to senior union representatives as well. One of the things they did was to have meetings at division and company level where trade union officials, shop stewards, could go off and meet the chairman of the company and members of the Main Board. That, I think, rubbed off on the trade union officials. There was a certain pandering to them that happened. So some of it was, I think, recognition of the inevitability of what was going on and another part of it was to neutralise them. ICI was fortunate also that I hardly came across a trade union representative who was working a wider political agenda.

(John Robinson, 1969-1989)

Nobody can kid you that democracy's easy because it isn't easy. It's very, very difficult. Instead of saying, 'Well, this is what you're going to do,' you have to say, 'do you think we should do this?' It takes a lot more time but it's important in my view. ICI recognised that because they made a lot of effort to get it together so that, on a monthly basis, the local area would have their own little meeting where they discussed with all the managers there - first time they've seen some of them - and all the shop stewards. They had an agenda and they could raise things. Maybe not mind-breaking subjects but still it was important to them. If you let the little things fester and then they grow and they grow and they grow then bump, you've got a major problem. In the early days they didn't trust the managers. I asked them why didn't they. Well, they didn't know anything about them. You see, they didn't see managers as workers. They thought they went to play golf every day and they didn't have families, anything like that. And it worked the other way. When I was doing a big job in ICI, I asked a number of managers the names of the shop stewards and whether they were married and most of them couldn't tell me. Didn't know what their hobbies were, whether they were gardeners or football fans. But if you'd asked the shop stewards the same they wouldn't have any idea because there was a vast gap between us, there was 'them' and 'us'. They had staff canteens, we couldn't go in them. There were workers' canteens. You could get somebody's daughter going at sixteen as a clerk and she'd have more privileges than her dad who'd been there thirty year, if he wasn't on staff grade.

(Dennis Carroll, 1952-1979)

By the 1970s the phenomenon of white-collar trade unionism was beginning to gather pace. I mean there were some flamboyant charismatic white-collar union officials. Clive Jenkins, I suppose, is the one that I remember most and they were beginning to gain a foothold in ICI, particularly in some groups where there were large numbers of Green Book people. People like draughtsmen for example and ICI could not cope, or did not wish to cope with that situation and certainly adopted widely different tactics to the tactics that it adopted towards the weekly-staff unions. I mean the weekly-staff unions were there, they were a fixture. They had to work with them. As far as the white-collar unions were concerned, my take on it is they didn't want them, they were going to keep their head down and not encourage them at all, not give them representative rights if at all possible and hope they would go away. ICI was lucky; they did go away because we had a change of government. We had a Conservative administration and they didn't feel anyway beholden to white-collar unions and it did fizzle out. But it was an indication to me that the senior management of the company were getting quite worried that there were people really quite close to them, almost people they see all the time. Weekly-staff people are down on the plant so to speak, white-collar people you pass in the office in the corridor. They were people who had got a different sort of agenda. And, of course, the white-collar unions began to ask about certain issues which the company preferred not to be surfaced. But that tide turned and they just fizzled out.

(John Robinson, 1969-1989)

Many of our senior shop stewards became full-time officials. It was quite a talking point that I would think at least half the full-time officials in the area had begun life as ICI shop stewards and because of the opportunity they'd had to develop in ICI. What they'd learned about how business ticks and what they'd learned about relationships with the management, that stood them in really good stead. I can think of six or eight of them who worked were full-time officials for many years on Teesside following the time as a senior shop steward in ICI.

(Robin Cook, 1961-1993)

Workers' attitudes to unions

He came in and he said, 'You'll all have to join the union.' I was the only one who spoke out. I said, 'Join the union? What do you mean?' He said, 'Well, all riggers, they've got a riggers' branch and they've got to join the rigging branch of the union.' So I said, 'Is there an apprentices' rate in this union then?' Where my mates used to pay about ninepence in old money, the tradesmen might have paid two and six, you see. And they said, 'Oh no, you've got to pay the same as the rigger.' I said, 'Well, we're not getting riggers' money so why should we be paying the same as the rigger?' I wouldn't join them. I've still got my paperwork now and anybody can look at it. And it wasn't to be clever. Five of them joined the union and I was the only one who wouldn't. Just before I was twenty-one, it's on my records at Transport House there, I actually joined the union. When I got through my test.

(Hughie Norman, 1958-2005)

Now when I came out of my time I didn't like unions because I thought the unions protected the incompetent and I believed that I didn't need the union. I believed that if they paid me what I was worth I would have got more than anyone else anyway. I was told when I come out of my time that I had to join the union. I was very reluctant. I kept putting it off and putting it off and then I was warned that if I didn't join the union I would be out which, I think, would be illegal now. Fortunately I'd gone one night down to the union and I said, 'I'd better fill this form in to join.' The following day the boss sent for me and said, 'If you hadn't got a union card or evidence that you're in the union.' I said, 'Well, actually I just went last night and signed.' They made me come home and get my union card. (Ginger Hawthorne, 1953-1964)

It finished up, where unionism, I think, really destroyed itself because the shop stewards had their own offices and then the shop stewards went round like lords and masters. And we were working for two supervisors. The supervision was that weak that you didn't know which side of the fence to sit on because you got a bigger bollocking off your shop steward than you did off the gaffer. (Barry Dunnill, 1956-1994)

Strikes

We were the biggest problem that ICI had - the riggers - in what they call now Human Relations, the Personnel. We organised a stoppage of work, all the group shop stewards, because of some problem. It must have been serious at the time and we picketed all the gates but we were sensible enough to allow what we called specialist people in like process operators. Some of them they couldn't have let them cool down so we allowed process operators who we picked, key personnel, just to go and let them tick over, not to produce anything of any significance but not to close it down. ICI were horrified. They would have shot me if they could, I think, because it had never happened before in all the history of ICI. Never had a dispute like that. It really did concern them.

(Dennis Carroll, 1952-1979)

Strikes were very unusual and ICI established with the unions a very sophisticated negotiating procedure which seriously significantly reduced the need for strikes to happen anyway. Not only were they a good employer but there was a very clear disputes resolution procedure which made it apparent that if you couldn't sort it out someone else further up the tree would sort it out for you. That happened on the union side as well as on the company as well. Both the strikes I was involved with were unofficial strikes. The issues had not gone through the negotiating procedures to the end point where the trade unions could legitimately call an official strike. They were well short of that and perhaps were showing a bit of the militancy that was happening in a wider national context at that time as well. The people were prepared to chance their arm a bit because they thought that they'd be successful if they did.

(John Robinson, 1969-1989)

You see unions are made up of their members and most union members felt about ICI as I feel about it. So, yes, they could fight the management, they could do all that but they didn't actually want to rock the ICI boat. On the other hand, ICI didn't want to rock the union boat. (Julian Phillips, 1956-1985)

Paternalism

I think originally it set out from cradle to grave. When ICI moved into Billingham there wasn't a Health Service so health provision would be primitive. But they put a lot of money into a plant, they put a lot of money into people and they wanted to look after them you know like the Rowntrees and the Terrys. This concept, 'These are our workers we'll provide them with homes, we'll provide them with this, we'll provide them with that, a health service'. I think that was the attitude.

(David Bryson, 1962-1992)

Paternalism wasn't oppressive, it wasn't limiting. It did have the side effect that most of your friends also worked at ICI. But the family feel was engendered by the fact that it was a pack of families there. Whether that would now count as fair, above board or inclusive, I don't know. What I do know is that it worked until outside events conspired to make the thing no longer viable.

(Julian Phillips, 1956-1985)

It looked after people, not only in a work setting but in a wider social setting. It was rather like saying, 'Well, we'll look after all your needs. We'll look after you, trust us. Give you a job for life, look after all your requirements. Sports, social activities, medical activities.' They even gave at one stage scholarships to ICI employees' children to go to university. I look back on it that we took away a lot of people's independence, a lot of people's freedom or need to take decisions for themselves. It created a dependency culture. When, of course, ICI caved in, as it did and I'm jumping ahead a few years now, it did cause shock, concern and alarm to many people who found it very difficult to adjust to a world where their employer was not going to look after everything. They'd got to look after things for themselves. Not a healthy situation in retrospect.

(John Robinson, 1969-1989)

In all of my time my sense always was that there was a very serious concern for the welfare of staff. Now that's not to be soft and fluffy and cuddly. That's not what I'm talking about. But I am talking about doing the right things and in the right kind of way so that there is sort of a mutual trust and respect. Paternalism means that when the company can afford to do things, the company actually did things it didn't really need to do. I really do believe that when the company was able to it tried pretty hard to do what it could. And that's why, you know, the Synthonia Club is there and that's why, even when it was a financial drain, it kept pumping money into it. It didn't need to do that for anything like as long as it did. There comes a time when no longer can you do some of these things. But it took care of pensioners and all those sorts of things. They were just terrific. That was the recognition of a very serious responsibility to local communities.

(Keith Farmery, 1970-2000)

The Green Room bar in the Synthonia Club.

Chapter 8

'Them and us' Relationships in the workplace

As we have seen in the previous chapter, ICI divided their workforce into weekly-paid payroll workers and monthly-paid staff with substantial differences in pay and conditions. After the Second World War there was growing unease about the inequalities perpetuated by this division. There were some minor changes made in the early 1960s which began to harmonize conditions of service. This process was enhanced by the introduction of MUPS and then WSA.

Debates about the inequalities between weekly and monthly staff conditions continued throughout the 1970s. At the Central Committee meeting at Harrogate in 1977, a representative from Ammonia Works pushed the question of harmonisation and argued that such differences 'kept alive the feelings of 'us' and 'them'.' He highlighted anomalies such as different holiday entitlements, the unequal length of working week and different retirement ages for weekly and monthly employees. The company personnel director at the time, Bob Haslam, recognised the continued existence of these historic differentials but promised further progress in the right direction.

The traditional distinctions between craftsmen and general workers on the plants were also reduced by MUPS/WSA. Craftsmen had traditionally served an apprenticeship where the skills of their trade were learnt and as a consequence they received higher pay. Unions who looked after their interests were always keen to retain these pay differentials in any negotiations with the company. This was reflected in disagreements over attempts to introduce the new pay scales under MUPS. The craft unions initially refused to be involved in the negotiations because they believed that the scheme reduced pay differentials and was more favourable to the general workers.

Status differences within ICI monthly staff were highlighted by job evaluation schemes and the convention of assigning employees into Books. The first company-wide job evaluation scheme for monthly-paid staff was introduced in 1963. All jobs below senior management level were evaluated on a 15 grade system named after Bob Haslam. Junior monthly staff on Haslam grades up to 10 were collectively referred to as Green Book staff. Those on Haslam grades 11-15, that is middle management and professional specialists, were Blue Book. Senior managers, Black Book staff, were graded above Haslam 15 and graded through a different evaluation scheme which ICI brought in from outside.

Not all staff assigned a grade within this system were on the same pay. Women had not achieved equal pay by this stage and this exposed another division amongst the workforce. The injustice of this situation began to be debated more regularly at staff conferences and joint consultation conferences in the late 1960s and 1970s leading up to the implementation of the Equal Pay Act in 1975. Up to this point it had been the company's policy that when women were employed in jobs that could be performed by men or women, they should only be able to progress to 80 per cent of the male salary. Women who had been with the company for more than five years and therefore demonstrated that they were 'career women' could progress to 100 per cent of the male salary but only at the discretion of management. This reveals the widespread view that most women did not approach a job as a career but as a stop-gap before marriage. The equal opportunities issue was also debated at the same time and the company set up a working party to report on the situation. It made a number of recommendations to improve the recruitment and progression of women and subsequent reports indicate gradual advances for women's employment opportunities. The majority of women, though, were still employed in the traditional female sectors of the industry such as clerical, administrative and catering.

Whilst the company's labour policies were partly responsible for the atmosphere on the factory floor, an account of these will not reveal the whole picture. Oral memories add an extra dimension to this story by providing personal perspectives on the culture of the workplace. This selection of extracts illustrates the relationships our contributors had with their fellow workers and managers.

Relationship with managers

You had to have man management skills and make the fellow feel as though he could come to you. You know, to talk to you. It was a bad manager or a bad supervisor if a fellow has two minds to come and see you. You went on courses to get them in. I mean lateness - you all went on one course and they were on about what would you do if it was persistent, somebody was persistently late and you asked them and they said they were sleeping in, could you get them an alarm clock. Well, this is true, this is true. Could we get you an alarm clock to get up? I mean this was ICI. It's crazy.

(Ronald Dowd, 1970-1990)

Power, that's it. Yes it is. A lot of it's power and that's the way they worked even at ICI. A junior manager said, 'No, no, we can't have that.' 'Why not?' I said. 'It's reasonable.' He said, 'Well, no, no, I'm just telling you.' But I got better at my job I realised that the poor sod didn't have the authority to do it anyway. But because he was a manager he had to keep that distance between him and me. Because he was much more important than I was. I was like a little raggy shop steward. Then it wasn't till I

realised that unless you talked to the guy at the top or the woman at the top, that's where the decisions are made. They didn't like me sometimes for it but I used to bypass them because you were just stalling with them.

(Dennis Carroll, 1952-1979)

In my book, they were outstanding. You know they were the top men. Their philosophy was plain to see. The way in which they handled even difficult circumstances. Shop stewards screaming abuse at them in the joint consultation meeting or something, never flinched, never turned away from that at all, always smiling, always coming back over and over again. I have immense respect for that as a philosophy and for the way in which they discharged it.

(Tony Brennan, 1955-1985)

Of course, from time to time you'd no doubt do things wrong and get your bottom kicked but he had a saying which was, 'If the learner hasn't learnt the teacher can't have taught!' He used to say that quite often actually. So he sort of accepted, I think, that if you made mistakes very often it was because somebody hadn't properly prepared you. So that made you feel slightly better.

(Robin Cook, 1961-1993)

I introduced my wife to the works manager and he introduced us to his wife and his wife turned to my wife and said, 'Do you have any children?' Margaret said, 'Yes, we have two.' And she said, 'And are they with you?' My wife, looking a bit puzzled, said, 'No we've left them at home.' Whereupon tall, elegant lady said, 'Oh, I meant were they away at school?' We turned away and Margaret said, 'What a fool.' I said, 'Tell you what love - it wasn't you that felt like a fool. There's no better answer to the question, "Are they with you?" than to say "well, of course not, we left them at home".' There was always a bit of that. I always used to think, by the way and I'm only going to say this because it's true, that the biggest status-conscious element of ICI were the wives.

(Tony Brennan, 1955-1985)

One of the mistakes that people make is to think that management is about telling people what to do. I just don't accept that. I think

Oil Works Long Service Dinner.

that's actually the wrong way round. I always thought that the role of the manager was to help people. By and large that stood me in good stead because people by and large seemed pleased to see me as opposed to not wanting to see me.

(Keith Farmery, 1970-2000)

I've got to be honest. When I first started for ICI I wasn't going to stay. I didn't like the systems they had. I thought they were too regimented in their systems and I wasn't used to that. It seemed as though the cliques were there and you had to get in with the clique and if you weren't in with the clique you were a rebel. Well, I wasn't in with a clique at all. Then they had their favourites, their blue eyes. I know the first set of overtime, I said to the assistant foreman, 'Excuse me but when are you going to ask me to work overtime?' He said, 'Oh well, when these lads don't want it, I'll ask you.' Well, I rebelled against that and I

went to see my manager and said to him, 'I think you'd better take my notice.' 'Oh, why?' And I told him, he said, 'Okay.' They had a book which you filled in to state your reason for wanting to leave. I wrote, 'I want to leave ICI because of the unfair methods especially in the distribution of overtime and jobs in the workshops.' He said to me, 'You can't do that.' I said, 'Well, is it untrue?' He said, 'Well, no but it's just not the thing to do. You know you'll never work here again.' I said, 'Well, to be honest with you, if I leave here I won't want to come back here again.' In that week he didn't submit the book to Personnel. In that week he got some of the people together and we had a meeting and decided that we would actually alter what they were doing and we would have a rota drawn up and everything would be done on a rota system so everyone got a fair crack of the whip.

(Robert Moran, 1966-1993)

On the engineering/production side we had a working party that had meetings every so often. They were run by me, the Site Director. But not to do with the Site but to do with looking for promising people and sort of starring them and getting agreement from maybe a couple of works managers. This then became your priority list for promotions, and in doing that, of course, you looked at all facets of him not just his bonus. But how he got on with people and how he managed people and how he got on with shop stewards and all this sort of thing. There was a similar one for the commercial people. We tried to reward the best people. It was never in any single person's gift.

(George Morgan, 1952-1982)

Hierarchy amongst workers

When you went in the Secretarial School you were immediately staff. That's because you'd been to grammar school and you had your O-Levels. If you went to secondary school and you wanted to start in ICI you went as a messenger boy, or messenger girl and then you took, if they'd deemed that you were good enough, a staff test at some time when you were maybe eighteen and if you passed that you were given a staff job. But when you went straight from grammar school with your O-Levels into Secretarial School you were staff straight away. But I think that it was good that it gave kids that didn't have a grammar-school education, it gave them an equal chance really. Because once they took their staff test and they passed they were the same as anybody else.

(Linda Flintoff, 1964-1976)

Now the significance between this Blue and Green Book thing was hugely important. If you were a graduate, almost whatever you did in ICI you entered the company at least at grade eleven which was the lowest grade in the Blue Book. When I arrived, I'm sure people in the Green Book were not allowed to become members of Norton Hall. There were attempts from time to time to chip away at it and that's why I think that people at the top end of the Green Book were allowed towards the end to become members of Norton Hall. But if you come from the Green Book you've not walked those hallowed corridors. You're different, you live in a different part of Billingham, you might live in a company house still. You wouldn't live in a company house if you were Blue Book by that time, apart from renting accommodation by people sorting themselves out. So I guess there was some resentment. I think it was latent and it never was very serious and I think people just accepted that was their lot. They acquiesced to that situation. I remember an occasion where a full-time union official retired, a very distinguished urbane well-respected man, ate his peas properly. We laid on a farewell dinner for him because we all regarded him as a really good bloke and we took him to Norton Hall. It was like winning the lottery. He said, 'I've never been in this place before, I've heard you lot talk about it all the time. I've never been allowed in.' It was like a portcullis was pulled up for someone like him and that was almost the greatest accolade we could give him that we could say to him come and have the dinner at Norton Hall. That little anecdote perhaps just illustrates. But he acquiesced to that situation. All the way through he'd not opened every meeting with a tirade of the iniquities of not being a Norton Hall member for weekly staff employees. It was just the way it was.

(John Robinson, 1969-1989)

I moved up the ladder in Work Study Department to be truthful. I became a technical officer which was Blue Book, more money and status. There weren't too many people in ICI who'd come in as electricians, made Blue Book. I can tell you that.

(George McGee, 1951-1985)

I wouldn't say I had a radically rocket-science-type career but I did pretty well in the Green Book grades and I got to the top of the scale in Green Book, through, I thought, quite hard work and sticking in and I felt it was recognised.

(Eric Collins, 1970-1976)

Crossroads Club at Hartburn.

Attitudes to women workers

You had to dress suitably for the office. Obviously on the wages we were paid, sorry salary, you couldn't afford to dress particularly smartly but there were rules. I do remember when cap sleeves first became fashionable we weren't allowed to wear those. You had to have sleeves that came further down. Not full length, perhaps above your elbow, but exposing that amount of arm was definitely just not on. And as for this current fashion for showing your cleavage and almost down to your belly button, that would not have been allowed. But what was funny, it was in the days of the 'sweater girl'. There was one girl in particular I remember, the men loved her and she was on the copy typing end. She wasn't anything but a copy typist so there she stayed. She used to knit these jumpers, ribbed, that clung and she wore a bra and I am not kidding you, her bosom used to end up almost under her armpits and she would sit there with it stuck out, typing away. She was a good typist, very quick. The men used to come in and they'd stand behind her shoulder with her typing away like this looking down upon this double mountain. I wouldn't have had the courage. I used to wear blouses and things, anything that showed my figure off. Oh, and that was another thing, you weren't allowed to go to work in the summer with bare legs and we had to wear stockings. It just wasn't the done thing. So if you went off and came back with a lovely suntan after your holiday, which we were starting to do then, you had to stick these blooming stockings on top of your lovely suntanned legs.

(Rita Nicholson, 1948-1966)

Women operating business machines.

There was a woman who'd had an awful lot of time off. So I said, 'Well, maybe I better have a word with her. She might need some help.' Because first thought is if she's having serious trouble the last thing she wants is to find that she loses her work because she needs it. But help can be given, we've got a Personnel Department who would be quite happy to come and see whether there's anything we can do. So I was all prepared to do that. I had her in a little desk there and a chair here and I'm sat like this and I used to pull the bottom drawer of my desk out and put my foot on it. So she's sat there. I met her, got up and walked her in, sat her down just there on the end of the desk. She wasn't behind the desk, she was just on the end nice and social and we're talking away and I put my foot on the desk like that. Talking away and she said, 'Do you mind? Do you normally put your foot on the table when you're talking to people?' I thought, 'Oh, bloody hell I'm getting a dressing down here.' I said, 'No, no, I'm sorry I didn't mean anything, I was just relaxed and I thought we were having a nice chat.' 'Well, I would rather you didn't if you don't mind.' Now that might

seem minor but it was something I hadn't even considered. I tend to do things in a relaxed way and if someone else is relaxing. What I had missed was that I was her boss and she took it as showing a sign of disrespect which I hadn't obviously intended but it alerted me to the kind of things which, in the order of things, are pretty minor but seemed to have a quite a significant effect in relationships.

(Ray Marriner, 1949-1985)

We got an apprentice girl in eighty-four/five, I would think. She was good, a marvellous welder and they say women have a nice sort of touch for welding. We lent her out to Metfab, a firm on Skipper's Lane, I think. She could only go on plants where there were ladies' toilets. So most of the work she did was in Research because women worked in there or in the canteens. And it was so limiting and at the end of it she went to be a nurse. Packed in, went to be a nurse. I said to the Apprentice School straight away, 'I don't want a girl apprentice, she won't like the job and at the end of the day all you've done is wasted an apprentice place.' 'No we can't sexually segregate, she'll have to come and do the job.'

(Mike Thompson, 1952-1990)

Women, they tolerate much more than men but once they lost it they were worse than men. They could really go to town and have shouting matches and everything. It was interesting because there was quite a few I looked after and 99 per cent of the time they were as gentle as lambs but that one per cent if something went wrong they were really vicious. It's difficult because the difference, of course, with women it's all emotion. They're easier to manage than men because they'll listen to you and they'll sort of apply more logic there. Men sometimes wouldn't take my advice, not because they didn't believe me but they wanted to prove how strong they were. Men saw everything as black and white, a lot of money was their value, the bonus wasn't right, whereas women didn't bother that much. They were more worried about the people who were looking after them or whether they were being treated fairly. Whether they should have got the job that somebody else got and there was always an ulterior motive why she got it rather than me and it was normally, you know, 'Ah well, she knows the male boss too well.'

(Dennis Carroll, 1952-1979)

When I went to tell the head one that I was going to be married in March fifty-four, she said, 'You must put in your resignation. Write it out and give it to me. You will have to leave.' I said, 'I want to keep on working.' 'Oh no, we don't employ married women.'

(Jean Miller, 1952-1954)

There was a new amenities block built in Research Department and for the first time the day-gang foreman was given an office instead of a wooden hut that he'd always occupied. He found himself in his new office next door to a similar office which was occupied by the lady chargehand of the cleaners. The language of the day foremen used to echo down the corridors. Whereas everybody was quite well aware of it, the chargehand lady cleaner, who came from a similar educational background herself, nevertheless chose to go to the day manager to complain about the language of the day-gang foreman. The manager, somewhat at a loss, decided that he, the foreman, would

have to apologise. So he told him that he was going to have to apologise and he brought the lady chargehand cleaner in to receive the apology. The large day-gang foreman drew himself to his full length and said, 'I have to apologise for my bad language but all I can say to you love is if I ever slip up again don't take any blankety blank, blank, blank notice.' And, hand on heart, that's a true story.

(Tony Brennan, 1955-1985)

We didn't have that many graduate women, although in later years, of course, we were very prone to wheel out our lady managers and engineers because they used to go round the schools on Teesside encouraging more girls to go in for chemistry, physics, engineering. I know we had two or three ladies particularly who got well known doing it. But it changed in the later years. There's a lady in the village here who is an engineer in Cassel Works at Billingham and doesn't think anything about that. So it is different now. Not necessarily equal, as it is in many professions, but there's a lot more now in management in the chemical industry.

(Robin Cook, 1961-1993)

Women packing urea sacks.

My husband worked at ICI as well. He was in Engineering Department. And when we got married I had to write a letter on my honeymoon to the company asking permission to stay on as a married woman. Now my husband didn't have to do that. That was 1964. There was a bit of uncertainty about whether we could both stay in the same department at the time. I suppose because of confidentiality. But in the end they let us stay in the same department and it was no problem at all. I just never discussed work with my husband.

(Patricia Whyman, 1957-1964)

There were a few carry-ons but you got through, you just laughed it off really. There were some fellows that would touchy-wouchy and you just ignored them.

(Betty Mitchell, 1957-1982)

Romance at the works

On one of my runs I used to occasionally do the second floor which was Distribution. There was a dark-haired girl there who said, 'How old are you?' And I said jokingly, 'I am sixteen or seventeen,' and she said, 'is there any more at home like you?' I had a brother in India at the time and so I set them up as pen pals. When he came back he married and Freda is our sister-in-law.

(Don Miller, 1943-1971)

I was working for his section manager at the time and, of course, I used to do the typing of the others when they came in. He did come into the office one day and said to me, 'I've got a little problem Rita.' I said, 'What's the matter?' And he was a gentlemanly man, he wasn't a rough sort of fella and said to me, 'I've got to come through to West Hartlepool on a certain day next week and I wonder if there's somewhere where I could perhaps, I don't want dinner, but somewhere perhaps where I can get something to eat.' There weren't many places to eat in those days. 'You know I wonder if you could take me somewhere,' sort of manoeuvring me, and in my total innocence I said to him, 'if it's a real problem I'm quite sure that my mother would be very happy to have you for tea.' He had always been so nice to me and he sort of took a step back, 'Oh, I'm

sure I wouldn't want to put her.....' I said, 'Oh, I am sure mum wouldn't mind somebody from work.' I'd done it for one or two of the girls for different reasons and that was it. I think he was trying to inveigle me into going out with him but without being devious about it. Afterwards I realised that I'd given him the perfect answer but I didn't realise it at the time.

(Rita Nicholson, 1948-1966)

Do you remember treasure hunts? You all went around and you had to find five horses in a row on the back of a barn or something like that. I think the police put a stop to them. In a little stream by Ingleby Greenhow she fell in. So I looked after her in the pub at Ingleby Greenhow afterwards. Then it was all very romantic. It sounds silly but there you are. It was a long time ago now. My boss had also got married at Billingham during the war so it wasn't really frowned on. What was frowned on was if you were in the same department, but I'd moved departments by then so that was alright. Same department, the woman would be moved obviously. I can understand that.

(Julian Phillips, 1956-1985)

Fun at work

This was Oil Works and Christmas. I was newish still and there were a couple of the tradesmen there. They made a Christmas cake out of lagging and they got a candle and wrapped it with the frilly paper. It looked good. All the top was covered with white stuff. It looked like icing. They had a raffle and a few tickets were bought and sold but not many. But it just so happened that one of the foremen, he was the senior foreman, had won, would you believe? So then one of the lads said, 'Frank you've won a cake.' 'Oh, great,' he said, 'can you take it up home for me?' He didn't want to take it outside. So we said, 'Yes, yes, we'll drop it off.' One of the other apprentices went through with it and went to the door and his wife opens the door. 'Oh, what's this?' 'Frank's won the Christmas cake in the raffle.'

(Ray Marriner, 1949-1985)

I only had recourse to their medical facilities once whilst I was there - a little accident in the lab. A rather hilarious end result but I got a face full of a chemical and we'll not mention the name of it just now because this is part of the joke. Apparently, ICI had a policy of people who were approaching sixty-five and weren't physically capable of doing a heavy job any more, they didn't throw them out, they found them a little make-work job somewhere just to keep them on until they were sixty-five. I went down to the nurse's station and she was out doing something. They had this old boy in there doing what he could and the treatment was perfectly okay. It was all in the book. Eyewash, etc, etc. Then, of course, there's the inevitable paperwork and he almost licked the end of his pen before he wrote it in and all the details, personal details and, 'What was this chemical you got in your eyes?' I said, 'Dibutyl phthalate.' Just a blank expression. 'How do you spell that?' 'D-i-b-u-t-y-l-p-h-t-h-a-l-a-t-e.' He wrote it all out and he looked up and he says, 'Couldn't you have got something simple like acid?'

(Allan Wilderspin, 1953-1955)

On the flat roof of the canteen changing rooms department there was some guys painting below. I got on the roof with a lump of string and a hook, lowered it down, hooked it onto his tin of paint and was lifting it up. As he was painting there, his tin of paint had gone. Daft things like that. But as apprentices you used to get jobs to do and tasks to do but they weren't strict on you, they weren't running about after you. Depending on where you were. Some places did. Another practical joke. An apprentice goes into the foreman's office. The foreman is deaf and he has a hearing aid. The apprentice goes in the office to see him for a rollicking and he starts lipping it without any noise from his mouth. So the foreman consequently starts to turn his hearing aid up, up and up. He still can't hear until somebody opens the door and busts in and speaks to him and nearly blows his ears out. You see daft things like that.

(Ginger Hawthorne, 1953-1964)

We had to do some performance testing on the CO_2-removal towers on Ammonia Avenue and that meant popping in and out all the time. The first time I went in I had to go down to collect some materials that had been left there by somebody the day before. I said to the lab superintendent, 'Will they let me in?' He said, 'Oh, you'll have to have a pass.' Now I'm absolutely certain in retrospect he was taking the mickey out of me something rotten because everybody wandered in and out like nobody's business. 'Oh, you'll have to have a pass,' he said and he very carefully wrote out on this little chit, properly printed chit which said, 'Please admit,' and he wrote in, 'One boy with bicycle.' He said, with absolute deadpan face, 'Show that to the man on the gate.' I was twenty-one at the time and I was going down to the CO_2-Removal Plant with carrier bag on the front of a bicycle to collect these samples and I had to show this bit of pink paper to the gateman, 'Please admit one boy with one bicycle.' He looked at it and he said, 'Have I to let you out again?'

(Tony Brennan, 1955-1985)

However, there was a slightly more laughable accident. There was an old tank, had been filled with phenolic tar - tar contaminated with phenol. Not strongly contaminated but in the end they cut the tank open to shovel this stuff out and knock it out with picks and there was a gang of labourers all kitted out like this. They worked away quite happily and got on with the job and then one of them when he came out for the rest period sat on a low concrete wall, took his PVC suit off and sat on the wall and suddenly realised he was feeling uncomfortable and everybody had been going in and out and had trodden on the wall and spread a layer of tar on the wall. He had sat on it and he had got a burnt bottom. He wasn't in any danger but it was regarded as rather humorous.

(Robert de Wardt, 1957-1981)

One of the other things that I certainly remember the draughtsmen doing, they used to love teasing the tea ladies. They used to come round with the trolley in the morning with coffee and tea. You could buy cakes and jam tarts and I think you could even have toast and biscuits and all sorts of things. They would have one of these jam tarts and when she wasn't looking one of them would slip up to the trolley and they would put a drawing pin in the centre of the jam tart and then when she offered it to them they pretended they couldn't pick it up because the pastry was so heavy. But I do remember years later, it would be way back when we got into the seventies and my husband used to come home very weary and say he had had a terrible day and I used to say, 'But it was always so much fun when I was there.'

(Patricia Whyman, 1957-1964)

Being telephone operators we used to deal a lot with dockets. What we called telephone dockets. That would have the extension number of the person's phone on and the information, the number that he wanted and details, all the details of the call. On the odd occasion, we would be a bit silly and fill one of these dockets in, pass it along and, of course, the operator would dial the number first you see. 'Hold on please. I have a call for you. One moment.' They would ring the extension number and say, 'This is your call.' So she would dial the number and ask for, 'Mr Lion,' and it would be the zoo. We would give her a zoo number and she would say, 'Oh, is Mr Lion there, please?' They would say, 'Sorry, pardon?' 'I'm wanting Mr...' And, of course, it would click because they would say, 'This is Chessington Zoo here or Regent's Park Zoo,' and she would say, 'oh, I'm very sorry,' and she would turn round and growl. So there were, you know, a few jokes. And also we always used

to answer the phone, 'Number please?' and when we sort of started to get a little bored we would go and answer, 'Rubber knees?' And they wouldn't know the difference between, 'Rubber knees?' and, 'Number please?'

(Rita Stafford, 1961-1991)

When we were in Research, I had a very, very badly cut finger there on a broken beaker. I've still got the scar. I ran in with this bleeding finger holding it tight and there was blood dripping out of it onto the floor. There was a queue and the nurse ran out and she said to me, 'That looks nasty, is it really urgent?' And I said, 'Not normally but I am a haemophiliac,' and she grabbed me by the head. 'Come in here quick,' and I said, 'I was only joking.' I would only be about seventeen, eighteen at the time and she gave me a right good smacking and she put this bandage on my finger. It was like a joke on the telly. It was a great big bandage out like that and she said, 'Don't you ever do that again.'

(Eric Collins, 1970-1976)

There were two fat lads, two very rotund lads and they would come walking up the road towards breakfast and I just happened to say, 'Oh, here's eighty-eight.' Another lad said, 'Who's eighty-eight?' I said, 'Two fat riggers - eighty-eight.' And after that it was always, 'Where's eighty-eight working?'

(Sean Booth, 1974-1994)

Research Workshops.

Chapter 9

'An alignment of interests' Benefits and facilities

The first chairman of ICI, Sir Alfred Mond, believed that providing extra benefits for employees would be advantageous to the company and help create a loyal workforce. In the 1920s state welfare was in its infancy and only provided basic necessities. In contrast, ICI offered its employees a vast array of benefits and facilities. They provided medical services, recreational and sporting facilities, company housing, canteens, share purchase schemes and a range of other services and amenities.

In the inter-war period ICI provided over 2,000 houses at Billingham. The company worked closely with Billingham Urban District Council and the Industrial Housing Association, a national organisation committed to improving the housing of workers. After building a modest number of houses near New Road, plans were submitted in 1929 to build about 1,000 houses north of Belasis Avenue. Building continued in the 1930s and a large number of houses were built north of the railway line and close to the station. The style of ICI houses varied to accommodate the diverse needs and income of employees. For instance, houses were erected at Norton for managers and for less senior staff at Mill Lane and Malvern Road.

Whilst these houses provided a necessary and welcome benefit to employees in the inter-war period, as incomes improved and the welfare system enlarged, the workforce became less reliant on ICI to house them. The company stopped their building programme and began selling their existing stock. After 1945 they relied on the local authorities to provide sufficient housing for their workers although they continued to subsidise 50 council houses in Billingham on condition that the tenancies were offered to essential workers. In 1967 all remaining ICI properties were sold to Bradford Property Trust, after first offering tenants the opportunity to buy the houses at preferential prices. They also continued to lend money to employees to buy houses.

Another progressive feature of the early labour policy of ICI was the Share Purchase Scheme. Most workers were entitled to buy shares at a preferential price and ICI also offered free shares to purchasers depending on their salary. A Profit Sharing Scheme was introduced in 1954 to increase the number of employees who felt they had a direct interest in the financial prosperity of the company. Employees received a bonus in the form of shares, with the amount dependent on the level of their pay and the profitability of the company in any given year. ICI had also established in the 1920s a Sickness Benefit Scheme, a Friendly Society, a Savings Bank and a Benevolence Fund, although some of these schemes closed in the 1960s as increasing numbers of employees could find similar and perhaps better services elsewhere. From the late thirties, the company also offered a contributory Pension Scheme which became compulsory for new employees in 1952.

As well as looking after the financial well-being of their employees, ICI also recognised that their physical health was extremely important. Medical services were launched in the 1920s staffed initially by nurses and employees trained in first-aid. Soon afterwards they began to employ full time doctors, physiotherapists, chiropodists, radiographers, and dentists and increased the number of nursing staff. They also built on-site medical centres. At Billingham, the medical centre was housed in the Grange, a former farmhouse used in the early days as the Main Offices. In 1960 a new main medical centre opened whilst Nylon and Cassel Works also maintained their own well-equipped medical centres.

One of the original aims of Mond's labour policy was to offer status and security for the workforce. Certainly, employment at ICI was prized because of the superior pay, working conditions, stable employment and the range of fringe benefits. This is reflected in lower than average labour turnover figures in comparison with other chemical firms. Long service was recognised by the company and presentation of certificates and gifts regularly took place in the Synthonia Club.

The Synthonia Recreation Club was formed soon after ICI bought the Site at Billingham and a brick club building was opened in 1931 by the company chairman. Employees could enjoy a wide variety of activities such as drinking, photography, football, cricket, boxing, drama and shooting. The social life of the whole community was enhanced by the facilities offered at the Billingham Site. Those not directly employed by ICI could join the Synthonia Club as associate members. The family of workers also enjoyed gala and visit days, outings, parties, dances and shows.

The Synthonia Club was open to all employees. Norton Hall was not and its membership was restricted to higher grades of staff. Its style and tone was said to be reminiscent of a gentleman's club or an Oxbridge college. Those allowed to join could enjoy fine wines, quality food and a range of sporting and recreational activities.

Most of those we interviewed felt this comprehensive package of benefits improved their working lives. To a large extent, ICI appears to have achieved its original aim of promoting a grateful and loyal workforce. The extracts below offer a flavour of thoughts on the wide variety of amenities available to those employed by ICI at Billingham.

Housing

I can always remember we came back up here and went into a house, a place called Sweethills, which is right next door to the old Sulphuric Acid Plant. It was only a couple of streets and it was hell. But it was only a holding place. It was all that was available at the time so we came into that accommodation and it was shocking. Black clocks in the morning in the fire grate and stuff like that. It was horrible. Black beetles. You know the black beetles about an inch long some of them. We called them black clocks. Well, we used to do. They were oldish houses and the conditions were really bad because the old Sulphuric Acid Plant did have horrid effluents. You could taste them, feel them, see them and Casebourne's was just over the other side of the road which was always cement dust so it was a pretty nasty place. Then when we came up to Central Avenue, we had an enormous garden. The rents were good, the houses were very good.

(Ray Marriner, 1949-1985)

There was a town of houses for people. Slightly hierarchical paternalism because at Billingham Bank there were houses for directors and over at Norton, Crooks Barn estate, they had houses for middle managers. Up Central Avenue, there were houses for foremen. Behind Central Avenue, there were houses for anybody. Nonetheless the company built houses for people at a time when there were no houses to be had.

(Julian Phillips, 1956-1985)

It was 1963 when I got married and we were living at the mother-in-law's house, which was a little bit overcrowded, in Middlesbrough. Anyway, it was my dad who told me about ICI houses if you could get one over here. If your engineer has a word he can get you updated on the list. So I'd put my name down for an ICI house but I was told it was a two-year waiting list. So I went into the engineer and I told him a few porkies. I said that I had fallen out with the mother-in-law. We were living there and she had told me I had to go in the next week and there's nowhere for me to go and I said this might affect me coming to work or not. So

ICI housing in Billingham, 1936.

he wrote me a letter. Well, he wrote a letter to the Estates Department of ICI which consequently led to me being offered the keys to a house the week after. So that's when I got the house.

(Barry Dunnill, 1956-1994)

As far as the housing side of things was concerned, I understand when the company first arrived here in the 1920s it built a wide range of housing for both blue and white-collar staff. By the time that I'd arrived there the houses that were built for the managers, they'd gone, they must have been sold. The housing that was available was for blue-collar workers and I guess the majority of those people didn't live in those houses anymore. The world had changed a bit. By the time you got round to the 1970s it wasn't a significant sort of issue.

(John Robinson, 1969-1989)

I can remember them coming round to see my father and this guy came round, official with his briefcase and such like. He said, 'Right, I've come down to see you. ICI will no longer have ICI houses in the near future.' He says, 'ICI are going to off-load them and sell them. It will be owned privately and you will be then a private tenant. So we're asking everybody, giving them the offer you can buy the house but we'll sell it to you cheaply.' So he said to my father, 'You can have the house for £700.' He said, 'You can't teach an old dog new tricks.' That was the words he said. We were all saying, 'Dad, you've got to buy it.' 'No, I'm not buying it,' he said, 'I don't want to know.' He said, 'I'm happy just renting it.' Anyway, we persuaded him and he said, 'Well, I'm not happy about it.' He moaned about it all the rest of his life. But when he came to sign the papers and they said, 'Right, the house is £900,' he said, 'hang on, you told me £700.' And they said, 'Yes, that was a year ago. That's what happens, the properties they keep going up in value.' He couldn't understand that. He thought if you had bought a £700 house, it was always going to be £700. Eventually he signed and he bought it. Then when he started paying the mortgage, he moaned about it for ages. He had to pay £7.50 a month mortgage.

(Dave Peacock, 1960-1972)

Shares

I think as a young man when I first got them as a single lad I blew them, it was a good way of getting some money quickly. Then when I got married it was, 'Ah, we'll save this year's and put them to next year's and that might help towards a car.' I think that's, in general, what we did. But I never ever saved up big blocks of ICI shares. I know people who worked with me who never cashed their shares. Good for them because when they retired they would have all those shares in their pocket. But I used it as a bonus, if you like. I never saved them up in big blocks, maybe two years or I think I once saved a three-year block for a new three-piece or something like that. But that's all we did.

(Roy Simpson, 1958-1999)

You get shares every year about Christmas time, every year you get your shares and it was a percentage of your salary until you got so many shares. I was always able to not spend it for a while and I used to leave the shares alone because we all thought that when ICI gave the shares out the price dropped. We thought the markets would recognise that there were a lot of these shares going about so they'd drop the price and most people, or a lot of people, used to sell them straight away. They wanted the money straight away or the wife wanted the money or something. Well, I never did that. I was always able to manage without cashing the shares in until they had gone up quite a bit. I was always able to wait until the share price had gone up and I would take advantage of a higher price and then sell them or there was something that I needed the money for and it coincided with the price being okay to sell them, instead of being dumped. These always went up.

(Dennis Oxley, 1955-1985)

Medical facilities

So the department had myself, it had two doctors; it had a couple of physiotherapists, part-time radiographer and, at one time, thirty nurses and several ambulance drivers. So that was developing and it was just a question of getting an efficient organisation. At that time, I think in this area, ICI was seen as a sort of an appendage of the National Health Service and we worked very closely with the GPs and with the local hospitals. For example, if we saw someone who, let's say, had diabetes or had sugar in his urine, we would check, he would come back into the department over the course of several days; we would check it and would tell him he had diabetes, gout, hypertension. I'd contact the GP and say, 'We've seen Mr 'X', he's got this condition, do you want us to send him to you or do you want us to refer him to the clinic at the hospital?' Invariably the GP would say that we could refer the person on behalf of the GP to the hospital. So there'd always be a copying letter and this system seemed to work very, very well for many years. I think we were seen as a benefit to the doctors. And, as I say, in all my time we never had a disagreement with the practices in the area, which was quite good.

(David Bryson, 1962-1992)

The medical was very good. Initially it was in the Grange which was a farmhouse on the original Site. Then when the centre got too big for the Grange they moved it across into a purpose-built building next door to the Labour Office and it was very good there. X-rays. They had a small minor operations room. You could go there for anything, any time. Also on that system was the blood-donor service which ICI allowed you to go to whilst still getting paid.

(William Hudson, 1951-1990)

I remember when I was having my first child. But if you had a slight headache or a pain you'd just go to the nurse and she'd lay you down and give you something cool on your head. It was a beautifully well-equipped little medical centre and nothing was too much trouble. She just had to say the magic words, 'No, I think you should go home.' And that's it. The nurse said I'd have to go home, so off you'd trot. You really, really were looked after. I've still got fillings now that I got at the dentist at ICI. They haven't budged. I think they must have got some secret ICI ingredient in them because every time I go to the dentist he tells me how good they are. You know they're really good. So that was what - thirty odd years ago? And I haven't had any trouble with them. But any need that you had they would look after you.

(Linda Flintoff, 1964-1976)

At the start of the apprenticeship you were taken round the Site. Other people would show you various things. Went to the medical centre and they had a full-blown operating theatre there. They had a morgue with eight places, in case any of the plant blew up. Its medical facilities were top notch. It was very, very impressive.

(David Sutheran, 1978-1982)

I did have a fall at the ICI. I fell out of the pipe bridge and I was taken to the ICI medical centre rather than going to the local hospital. They dealt with me pretty well. ICI's own ambulance took me to the medical centre and I found out I had broken seven ribs plus bruising and what have you. So they dealt with me in there. Doctor and the nurses they had in there and they dealt with me. In those days they used to strap you up. So they did that and they brought me back home in their ambulance.

(Eric Christie, 1953-1983)

I had a problem with a cartilage in 1973, had an operation on a cartilage but prior to that I'd seen my own local doctor. He said, 'Really, you need some exercise before your operation to keep your muscles right.' Because then you were laid on your back for eleven days after a cartilage operation. He said, 'I'll have to get you in for some physiotherapy.' I said, 'Well, can I do it at work?' He says, 'Where do you work?' I said, 'ICI.' 'Oh, better than I can get you, just go to ICI and let them do all the pre-work for us,' which I did. The medical was advanced, wasn't it?

(Roy Simpson, 1958-1999)

When I was thirteen I contracted a disease called Bright's disease and I was given up as a no-hoper. I was dying. There was a new doctor came into Billingham. The long and short of it was he saved my life and my father, who was working in ICI then, got me away to Grange-over-Sands convalescent home for a fortnight through the ICI. I don't know whether it was solely for ICI or whether they contributed to the cost but I went for a fortnight's convalescence to Grange-over-Sands.

(Bob Tucker, 1937-1949)

Sport and hobbies

I didn't play tennis or football or cricket or rugger with any of them but we had a Wireless Society. We went to hear lectures on the wireless of those days because everybody was interested. All young men were interested and the ladies, too, in the crystal sets. And valves.

(Kenneth Warne, 1922-1968)

We were also encouraged to go to the sporting complex belonging to ICI where they used to teach us to box and do physical training because they thought we were emaciated. We used to get Horlicks tablets and National cocoa to keep us strong.

(Don Miller, 1943-1971)

There's one thing that was a little unusual. I had been there about four or five weeks and a phone call came for me from the firm's PTI [Physical Training Instructor]. Why hadn't I been turning up for my hour and an half's PT a week? I said, 'Well, basically because I didn't know anything about it.' He said, 'Well, you have to be there on a Friday at ten thirty,' and told me exactly where it was. It was part of the big field next to the Synthonia Club. You'd do a few little exercises to warm up and he was teaching us all judo. We were throwing each other around the mats with gay abandon and highly enjoyable. And because I was fit to start off with it didn't mean a great deal to me. It wasn't an effort; it was something new I was learning. Every four or five weeks when you were all starting to get a little bit cocky because you could throw each other all over the place, he would line you all up and say, 'Right, the first three come and get me.' The first three would dash in and the same three would fly out a few nanoseconds later. Highly bruised egos. The next three and he would go right along the whole class until he had flattened the lot of us and then say, 'You've learnt a lot but you haven't learnt enough yet. Shall we carry on gentlemen?' It was a thoroughly enjoyable time.

(Allan Wilderspin, 1953-1955)

They wanted everyone to be happy in work and out. They provided the ICI Club, the Synthonia Club which they built and a stadium opposite.

Gymnastics on the Synthonia Junior Club field.

Any sort of activity you wished to do, providing it was sensible and practical, they would endorse it and back it and finance it. I used to swim for the Machine Shop's team. I used to play cricket for the Cement Works' team. I played ten pin bowling for the Cassel Works' team. I used to go down to the ICI gym and I used to train on the weights in their gym. And then some of the lads that came in were happy to have a game of five-a-side football in the gym. We were the originators of the ICI Potholing Club. I first started hiking there with one of them. They had the ICI Club there. Sometimes I could go and meet my pal on a Thursday night and we'd go down to have a game of snooker and a couple of pints of beer. But sometimes when I'd been in the gym because it was only across the road from the stadium, I would walk across the road after I'd been to the gym and go in there for a drink after work before I went home.

(Dave Peacock, 1960-1972)

But there was a Billingham Synthonia Recreation Club and there was a social section which you could join. There was cricket, tennis, table tennis. I used to have a handicap so large that after two points I would win the game. So that's how high my handicap was. There was swimming, archery, rifle shooting and lots of opportunities for men and women to join the social club. You would pay so much a month out of your wages.

(Rita Stafford, 1961-1991)

Billiard room in the Synthonia Junior Club.

The tennis courts were very popular for friendly games and inter-departmental competitions.

The gardens at the rear of Norton Hall.

Norton Hall

You had to be a certain grade. Before I actually joined one or two people said, 'They don't have a tennis club, you know. They only play the occasional tennis.' Most of the people that played in the tennis club were Synthonia, can't go to Norton Hall. So I realised then it was elitist and that's not part of my make up. So I didn't join and I never joined.

(Dennis Oxley, 1955-1985)

Norton Hall Club started in the 1920s. Wilton Castle Club started in the 1940s and one of the natural things was to create bars which were used by people in the early days both at lunchtime and the evening. Learning about good food, having dinners, having entertainment, having balls and dances, having smokers and all these sorts of things. Every one of those involved alcohol in one form or another. So the bars had to be run, the wine had to be purchased and that was all done by the clubs and for the members. That history existed so I joined those activities and very soon got involved myself in leading them.

(Brian Deans, 1957-1993)

Norton Hall butler in the 1930s.

It was a five-star hotel and I suppose you would describe it as like a gentlemen's club. Everyone from plant engineer, that level up, were members of Norton Hall and it had tennis courts and so on. But it had suites of rooms and visitors would come and use the bedrooms and they would stay there. Dining could be quite elegant because we were entertaining our customers. At dinner the waitresses would bring in great salvers with beautifully cooked food and you just selected your own meal. The quality of the food was five-star. When you were introduced to the company you stayed at Norton Hall for a week or two - or was it a month? It took a bit of getting used to. I came from a very happy, very secure home but we certainly didn't have the standard of life that we now enjoy. We didn't travel, we didn't go abroad. I found myself encountering people who had done all of these things and I was sort of thinking, 'Oh, how do you fit into this?' But with the gradual exposure that ICI gave you it just became natural.

(George McKinlay, 1957-1985)

Synthonia Club

The social life was quite good because you used to have the dances in those days, the Research dance and things like that. So every now and again we used to have these social events at the Billingham Synthonia Club and they were major events. Barbara used to put on her satin dresses and things like that and used to get properly dressed up for the occasion. You couldn't go along in jeans or anything like that. This was formality at its best.

(Alf Illingworth, 1952-1969)

The ICI Club, as we knew it, the Synthonia Club, was a wonderful place to be. You could go in at half past four because the law said pubs could open at half past five so you had an hour's start. It was a place where you could meet. We had many of our shop stewards' meetings there. Sometimes you can overdo it so I'd say, 'Look, we'll have a half hour meeting after work.' You'd go to the ICI Club and have a pint and off you'd go after the meeting. But there was a lot of activity going on, so many

The Synthonia Club built in 1931 and restored in 1956 after suffering bomb damage in the war.

The main bar in the Synthonia Club.

things to do. I didn't use it regularly because I lived in Norton and it was in Billingham but more than often I'd go after work. I would go in the evening sometimes if there was a function on, a presentation of some sort or some darts thing, whatever it was. Or our works would be playing another works in indoor sports, dominoes and darts. It was a good night. You know, people really relaxed then. In fact, if I'd have lived nearer I would certainly have been a more regular customer. It cost us tuppence a week.

(Dennis Carroll, 1952-1979)

I was chairman of Synthonia for a while. I didn't go regularly as in every day or every week or every Friday or at a particular time. But it was there and we would regularly say, 'Right, let's go and have a half an hour's unwind,' at the end of the day or something

like that. I personally never thought of it much more than that. Then in the eighties, I was asked to go onto the committee. Someone said, 'It's good training for you, young man,' or something pretentious like that. So I did as I was told and then I became chairman for a couple of years. There were two or three management appointees. The treasurer was a management appointee; the chairman and the deputy chairman were both company appointees. I think the chairman of the sports section was also a company appointee. But apart from that, yes, there was the manager of the club, there was the general secretary of the club and then there were the committee members. Now the committee members were elected by members of the club in the time-honoured fashion. You stood for it and got elected if they liked you and not if they didn't.

(Keith Farmery, 1970-2000)

The Brown Room, a men-only bar when first opened.

Entertainment

The Research Party would run for an hour and a half with an all amateur cast drawn from Research and the songs would be about Research and its top men and its lesser men and its mistakes and everything that it had done. The very first time I appeared on that party there was an item which referred to the introduction of vending machines in the Research Department. Prior to that, the waitresses from the staff canteen during the day would serve coffee in all the offices. They'd come round with a trolley and you got a cup of coffee and a biscuit if you wanted it. Then they decided they would have vending machines instead and I was given this monologue to perform with a piano accompaniment. And the first verse said:

There are automatic tea machines in 'W' and 'Q',
And another near the ice machine in 'D',
Where insertion of a dodecahedral threp'ny bit,
Brings a pseudo cup of automatic tea.

There was another crazy verse. It's amazing how memories come flooding back from twenty-five years ago:

They also did opinion polls amongst the rank and file,
Unanimous the staff reaction came,
And as in other matters where democracy prevails,
They carried on regardless just the same.

We used to get senior managers from other divisions, from Personnel Department in London, from the Main Board. They always came up for the Norton Hall smoker. It was that famous. But also quite a few of them turned up for the Research Party as well. I came down off the stage on one occasion and a very senior terribly, terribly educated gentleman from where I know not said, 'Oh, you should be in the Norton Hall smoker.' I said, 'I would if you paid me enough to qualify,' or words to that effect. And, of course, with a bit of inverted snobbery when I eventually broke through that barrier and got myself into the ranks of the management and professional staff in Personnel Department, I took it upon myself to say, 'Well, if they made me wait for fifteen years they can wait for another bloody fifteen years.' So I never did join Norton Hall.

(Tony Brennan, 1955-1985)

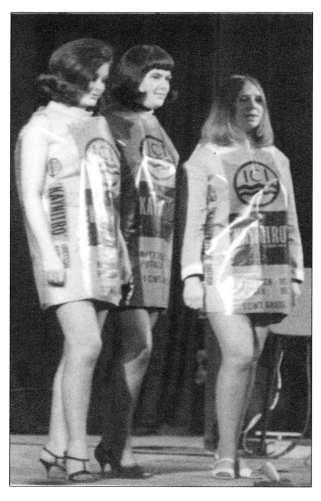

Research Party in 1967.

I joined the drama section and I was part of Synthonia Players for as long as they were there in the Synthonia Theatre until I remarried. Then I had two children and I did a couple of shows I think but after that it sort of petered out. My main interest was the drama section. The Synthonia Players did plays and once a year they did a revue and then they branched out into pantomimes. So we did a fairly wide range. I mean drama within ICI in those days was very strong, the Research Department particularly. They used to put on this Research Department revue every year. But it was only open to members of Research Department and therefore you didn't get to see it if you didn't work in the Department. Very Very clever. Entirely in-jokes. Some of the others started to write for the Synthonia Players and that was when I joined because I wanted to be in the revue.

(Rita Nicholson, 1948-1966)

They did this Norton Hall smoker once a year and, of course, all the directors used to go and I think they used to invite some from Head Office as well. It was always terribly highbrow and, of course, Black Book members could apply for tickets and go. It was all very highbrow and very, very clever. Very clever indeed. They had some wonderful writers, they really did. For a long time they never had women in it and then they did invite a couple. Nobody knew what was in the Norton Hall smoker because it poked fun at all the top-notch men. Except the girl who did the typing and she would be shut up in a small office to type the Norton Hall smoker. It was like the state secret, nobody was allowed to see it and she had to swear not to tell anybody what was in it which made us all the more keen to see what it was. I did get the chance in later years to hear a little bit of it on the quiet. But there was an enormous range of talent within ICI.

(Gwen Mountain, 1956-1960)

We were working with the plumbers. And then they said, 'Do you want to buy a ticket?' I said, 'What for?' They said, 'We're having a smoker, it's a shilling a head.' 'Yes, I'll go,' and I said, 'but what's a smoker?' 'Oh,' he said, 'we have it in the Turk's Head at Stockton.' The back room, they hired the back room and it was like a sing-song. Then our secretary said, 'We'll have a smoker.' He said, 'We'll have a smoker.' I said, 'Where?' He said, 'The Cricketers, Portrack. We can hire a room upstairs.' We went up there and we had a riggers' smoker and that was the start of it. Just for riggers.

(Jimmy Cutter, 1940-1978)

I met my wife playing tennis in the Distribution inter-section tennis tournament and people came to the theatre who played. There were revues and the revues were a very high standard and very cutting. The sort of things Stalin would have chopped people's heads off for and the directors had to sit in the front row and laugh.

(Julian Phillips, 1956-1985)

We did have a Distribution dance one year but it was singularly awful. I've never forgotten it. Some of the men got drunk and they tried to be over-familiar. Oh, I used to loathe it at Christmas because of this. I can remember

Synthonia Theatre, 1956.

going to hide in the ladies' cloakroom at one stage when they all came back having had a bit too much and thought that you were all sitting there waiting to be pawed which I objected to very strongly.

(Rita Nicholson, 1948-1966)

Outings and Gala Days

When I was working at Billingham and when the kids were very, very small we had works outings to places like Flamingo Park and Whitby for the day and that sort of thing. We used to go there as a family. We went to the pantomime. There was an organised pantomime trip to Stockton to the Hippodrome. I can remember we went for two or three years with the kids.

(Jim Steedman, 1946-1987)

One of the sections in Engineering Department, the Civil Structural and Architectural Section, had a social committee. They used to organise, in the summertime, buses and we used to go out and go walking on the North Yorks Moors and all over the place. People used to bring their families with them as well. They used to organise dances and treasure hunts and various things like that. And also when I was first in the typing pool the whole of Engineering Department used to have a Christmas party for the children.

(Patricia Whyman, 1957-1964)

We used to have an annual Sports and Gala Day. I think it was July every year. They were all at the cricket field and they used to get international runners in. I remember one of the four-minute-mile men coming to Billingham and running an invitation race. There were inter-departmental competitions from the various works which would have a team and they would have running. They had children's races. They had cyclists competing in cycle races. I think they used to start on a Saturday afternoon about one o'clock and go on till about five or six. I remember going to those both before I started working and after I started. I went with my father and my mother and we all went and had an afternoon out and then I remember going along in my own right and seeing these competitions. But they were big events in the early days of ICI and into the

A works outing.

ICI Christmas party.

fifties I would think, probably well into the fifties. I can't remember when they stopped. I think they stopped when people had cars and it no longer became something to do. You know people would say, 'Oh, we're going shopping or we're going to the football match,' and they would be going here and going there.

(Jim Steedman, 1946-1987)

Long Service Awards

We had Long Service Award functions and we'd hold probably four a year. At each of those Long Service functions there might be a hundred recipients or something. They'd be there with their wives and they'd be receiving awards for twenty, thirty, forty years, whatever. There were always two personnel officers on duty. The awards would normally be presented by a member of the Division Board. If there were high-level managers of the division itself receiving awards then there would be a Main Board director who would be doing the presentations. One personnel officer's on the microphone and he would call out the name and the works and the length of service of the next recipient and that recipient would come forward to receive his award. The second personnel officer is standing at a table which is covered by all the awards that are going to be presented, each one with a little ticket on with the man's name. And as the man's name was called, and you all had to be careful in case the personnel officer on the microphone missed a name out and went to the next one, the second personnel officer would identify that particular award, pick it from the table and as he handed it to the presenting director, he would whisper something in his ear. Like, 'Bill is a chrysanthemum grower and has won awards.' As Bill arrived and the director held his hand out to shake his hand he'd say, 'How are the chrysanthemums this year, Bill?' Bill would go back to his table with his eyes like organ stops and say, 'How did he know that I grew chrysanthemums?' We used to call that 'whispering'.

(Tony Brennan, 1955-1985)

Long Service Award Dinner. Presentations were given for 20, 30, 35 and 40 years' service.

They made a big thing of it. People were getting twenty-year awards, thirty-year awards and up over. On the same night. They would offer you what we would call a catalogue nowadays and you picked out what you wanted. A wristwatch, a watch, other clocks, panel piece clocks. I picked a wristwatch. I've still got it. The event was quite a big do. There was a drink. Obviously you had things to drink and meals and what have you, photographs and it was in the Synthonia Club. It must have been a good do because we still remember it

(Eric Christie, 1953-1983)

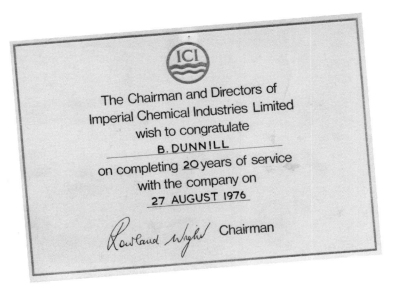

The Chairman and Directors of
Imperial Chemical Industries Limited
wish to congratulate
B. DUNNILL
on completing 20 years of service
with the company on
27 AUGUST 1976

Rowland Wright Chairman

An example of a Long Service Award Certificate.

Retirement

There was a collection made. The collection included a little book with signatures of people that had... well, I am not sure whether they all contributed to this collection. But they signed it anyway and, 'All the best,' and this sort of thing, you know. It was normal in departments. I would imagine it's normal in most departments. It was normal in the Engineering Department and I have a book now of people who signed it and so I can go back and look at it once in a while, you know and, 'Oh, yes, I remember him. Who was that fellow?' You know, scratch my head and think.

(Dennis Oxley, 1955-1985)

When I retired in 1985 I remembered saying to the then division training manager that the training that we had provided up to that point for people who were retiring and which I'd attended, was - quote - 'the worst training I have ever been subjected to in my life and if we can't do better than that we want shooting.'

And he came back with the obvious answer, 'Well, can you do any better?' From 1985 to 1995 I ran two-day financial planning courses or prep for retirement courses. I ran those courses for ICI. When I started running those courses he probably thought I was going to do four a year, one a quarter, with maybe ten people at a time including wives or husbands. In the late eighties we'd taken the Research lecture theatre and had opened it up for weekly staff to attend as well and I was running courses once a month with as many as ninety people at a time. In one respect, I was enjoying the peak of that activity whilst recognising that it was the worst period that I'd seen ICI go through and were shedding jobs like nobody's business.

(Tony Brennan, 1955-1985)

I do know that pensioners could go to the canteen at Billingham and have a subsidised meal. Obviously they weren't working at that stage but the company did still look after them.

(Shirley Cooke, wife of George Cooke)

George Morgan making a retirement presentation on Gas and Power Works in the 1960s.

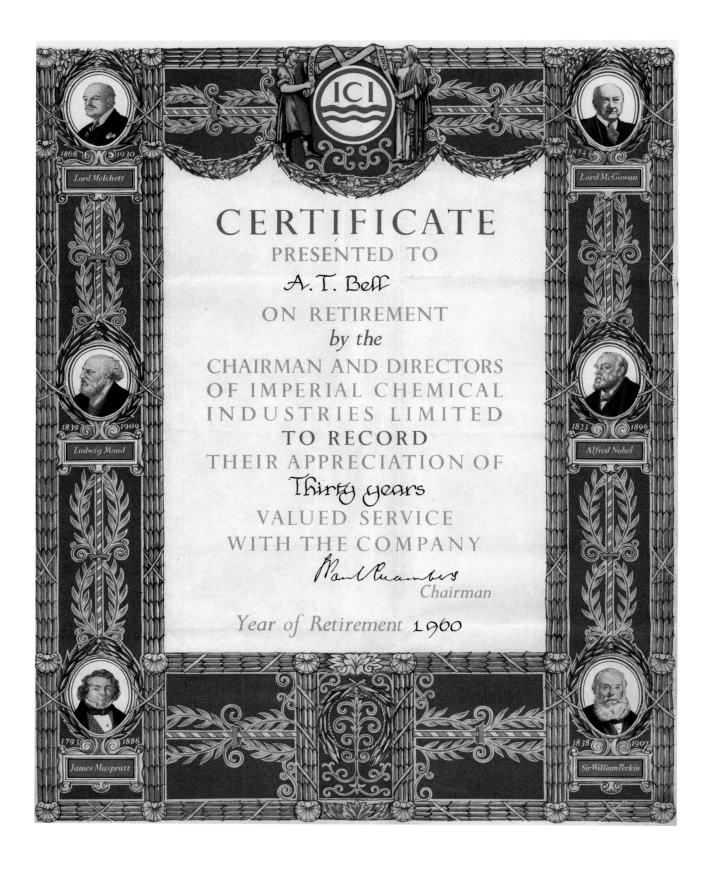

An example Retirement Certificate.

Getting to work

When I say 'a mass exodus', I mean it. Bikes, nothing but bikes coming out of the gates. You could stand at the top of Billingham Bank and all the men would come pedalling like hell through Billingham, past the picture house, top of Billingham Bank. They'd all freewheel and they'd all be going at the same speed. You could stand there and all you could see right across Billingham Bottoms right up to Beaconsfield Road was a mass of black objects. You couldn't see the road for bikes and do you know I can still see that now even after all this time. It was a marvellous sight. There must have been thousands of bikes, cyclists on that road and it all just whizzed down Billingham Bank and just freewheeling across the Bottoms.

(Bob Tucker, 1937-1949)

ICI used to be like Holland in there. There were more bikes than anything else.

(Tom Boumphey, 1944-1987)

I also have very vivid memories of the West Gate being closed at four o'clock and that hooter that used to go to signal the end of the working day. Some unfortunate bloke had to open that gate and an absolute torrent of men on bicycles and running for the buses, poured. Just completely flooded the road. All the Stockton Corporation double-decker buses were trying to do three point turns round the war memorial before the bus station was built.

(Tony Brennan, 1955-1985)

The amazing thing was in the morning and in the evening when people used to come to work, outside the main building was a massive bus station and then you got buses coming in from the four corners of Cleveland - Teesside if you like. Coming in and picking up all these workers from ICI. It was a major logistics exercise.

(Alf Illingworth, 1952-1969)

Workers leaving the West Gate in the 1950s.

Empty buses going up Chiltons Avenue to take workers home from the West Gate.

Catering facilities

There were the workmen's and the staff canteens and then every division in ICI had its own. A dining room and the workmen's canteen filled up loads and loads of food and delivered it to various elements of ICI. They shipped all this food out in hundreds and hundreds. It was probably maybe a thousand, one and a half thousand meals each shift. The staff canteen had two shifts. I can't remember whether it was half past twelve till quarter past one. But they ate in two shifts and probably a hundred or a hundred and fifty per sitting.

(Jean Owen, 1941-1945)

The senior staff had a restaurant with waitress service. The service existed for several years and it was a bitter disappointment when the personnel director came along and said we were going to suspend it. I persuaded him to keep going for another twelve months on the basis that most of the people that went for lunch ended up talking shop for the whole of the hour. This was above the main dining room for the general staff.

(Gill Bowness, 1956-1991)

ICI was a highly hierarchical organisation in those days. Very highly hierarchical. I could talk for a long time about that. To take a very simple example, there were six levels of staff dining room accommodation. Starting at the top there was a chairman's dining room where he could take his favourite guests and when he wasn't using that he joined his fellow directors in the directors' dining room. There were two levels of monthly staff dining rooms. There's the staff dining room itself and a rather higher level with rather difficult to define requirements for you to go up to it. You were invited and it was an invitation. Now you come down to the weekly waged and they had a set of dining rooms. Then there were the brush hands who were the lowest of the low. Not because they were particularly regarded in the hierarchy as lower than the unskilled daily people but they got a bit dirtier. So they had a separate room. So you had six levels of dining.

(Alf Rout, 1940-1977)

We had subsidised meals in the canteen. And a very good meal it was - for your nine pence. It cost everybody nine pence in old money. We got the same menu each day as the main canteen where all the office workers went.

Staff canteen.

It was just the surroundings weren't quite so salubrious. We had the same food. Everything was clean but it was rough wooden tables instead of nicely set out tables.

(Allan Wilderspin, 1953-1955)

This was remarkable because there are two things. First, the tea girl used to come round and they used to have these big kettles of lovely hot milky coffee. But I also remember thinking, 'Isn't this really nice to have a nice cup of coffee in the morning and tea in the afternoon, all delivered by the tea girl?'

(Alf Illingworth, 1952-1969)

He used to do two till ten, ten till six and six till two. If he ever worked overtime that was best because he used to bring snack boxes home that the ICI gave them. Fantastic. We used to eat it because there used to be all sorts of little tins of baked beans with sausages and we just didn't get them. We used to raid his snack boxes. He used to bring them home for us.

(Anne Boyes, daughter of ICI employee)

There was always a crowd of children round the West Gate and as you came out they all said the same thing to you, 'Have you any bait left, have you anything?' This was before the war and you'd always have a crowd of bairns. I wasn't allowed to do it. My father would have killed me. My father's bait used to be wrapped in newspaper then tied into a red handkerchief. There was a hell of a lot of men used to sit down for their dinner in the ICI between twelve and a quarter to one. They'd make their tea in the can. They'd open the red handkerchiefs and open the newspaper and eat the sandwiches. There was a hell of a lot of them used to deliberately not eat the last sandwich, used to keep it for the kids going out.

(Bob Tucker, 1937-1949)

Shop

It started off, as I remember, as a place you can go and get 'floor sweepings' as they were called from the fertilizer packing sheds. You would get Nitro-Chalk and you could get CCF and they would put it into stone bags, into fourteen pound bags. This gradually expanded until they were selling things, again at reduced prices and sodium hypochlorite which is like Domestos, I think. The basic materials for making Sqezy, you know the washing up liquid, which came from Oil Works, you could buy that. And then as time went on and part of ICI went into the market selling these fertilizers you could get pre-packed lawn foods and the spreader, all at reduced prices and other garden implements and tools. Initially it was only open for certain hours like half past four till five or half past four till half past five. But after a while I seem to remember the garden shop became open to anybody who wanted to use it. It wasn't just for people who worked at ICI because it was situated outside the works gate, outside the West Gate, so that they had a guy from Supply Department who ran that and anybody could go up. But the shop where they sold the clothing was, if I remember rightly, either inside or just outside Chilton House.

(Jim Steedman, 1946-1987)

Norton Hall's main dining room.

Chapter 10

'Incendiaries and high explosive' ICI at war

The Second World War posed numerous challenges for ICI. Many of their products were essential to the war effort and the Billingham Site was clearly going to be important because it produced a range of chemicals which the Government needed. At the start of the war, it was the only ammonia factory in the country. A large amount of synthetic ammonia was needed for fertilizers to increase food production and was also used in the production of explosives. In view of this, the Government felt that the Billingham Site was too vulnerable to attack from German bombers and ICI agreed to build essential plants elsewhere. For example, ammonia plants were opened at Mossend in Scotland and Dowlais in South Wales.

The company created detailed plans to defend plants and people in the event of war. They trained employees to serve as volunteers in ARP (Air Raid Precautions) units in factories. Plans to evacuate staff from head office and other densely populated areas were finalised. At Billingham, some office workers and researchers were evacuated to outlying areas like Yarm, Hartburn and Norton. Employees started to build air raid shelters and dig trenches. Brush hands (industrial painters) blacked out and camouflaged buildings. Decoy sites were arranged in neighbouring areas and smoke screens were prepared to disguise plants. At the outbreak of war barrage-balloons were positioned above the factories and neighbouring houses to foil attack from low-flying aircraft.

Inevitably, there were some bombing raids on the Billingham Site. In 1942 it was hit by incendiaries and high explosives causing numerous fires. In July of the same year an oil tank was hit causing the loss of about a million gallons of petrol. One employee was killed in this raid. Houses surrounding the Site were also badly damaged.

Many ICI personnel were directly involved in the war effort. Leading scientists and technicians were used in overseas missions to improve war production in Canada, Australia and Africa. Government departments drew heavily on the skills of senior executives and administrative staff. Large numbers of the company's employees joined the forces. In 1939 over 1,500 men from Billingham Division had enlisted and this had risen to about 3,000 by 1945. Naturally, this entailed recruiting large numbers of men and women to cover gaps in the workforce and maintain production levels.

By 1945 there were almost 2,500 women employed at Billingham. Many still worked within traditionally female sectors such as clerical, secretarial and catering. However, they were also now employed as process operators, fitters, welders, crane drivers and in other unskilled or semi-skilled jobs. Most were employed on the understanding they would give up these jobs when the men returned at the end of hostilities.

This was obviously a difficult operating period but production at Billingham actually increased and the Site continued to supply a range of essential products such as Nitro-Chalk, CCF, ammonia and sulphuric acid. It also increased the manufacture of Perspex for use as glazing in aircraft cockpits and the Petrol Plant at Billingham produced high-grade aircraft fuel.

Billingham was also heavily involved in the development of 'special weapons' on behalf of the Government.

The Engineering Department built a powerful anti-tank weapon which became known as the Blacker Bombard. They also helped design and produce the PIAT (Projector Infantry Anti-Tank) Gun. This was a light gun with the capacity to pierce tank armour. The Government ordered 115,000 PIATs and the workforce were able to complete the contract seven weeks early. Billingham scientists and engineers were also entrusted to work on secret research into the development of an atomic bomb, given the code name 'Tube Alloys'. They were able to design a gaseous diffusion plant to separate uranium 235, the bomb's explosive material, from pure uranium, but political developments led to Britain taking a minor role in the subsequent development of the first atomic bomb by the Americans

Working conditions during the war were demanding but it was essential that morale was maintained. ICI helped employees by compensating for the higher cost of living during the war, paying a war addition bonus of nine shillings for men and seven shillings for women. They did not forget the men who were fighting in the forces. Enlisted personnel were entitled to retain their membership of the pension scheme and ICI paid married men the difference between their service pay and salary.

Workers' morale on site was strengthened by regular ENSA (Entertainments National Service Association) concerts in the main canteen. Talent contests, comedy and film shows were organised amongst workers and the company kept the sporting and other recreational facilities open. Sporting heroes, politicians and royalty visited Billingham to promote support for the war effort. The highlight of these undoubtedly was the visit in 1941 of King George VI and Queen Elizabeth, reflecting the importance of the Site to the country.

Only a small number of those we interviewed worked during these war years but they have a fascinating and dramatic story to tell of this unique period in the history of the Billingham Site.

Defences

When the war started, the Research Department was evacuated to Hartburn. They were still making ammonia and working on producing motor fuel. At one time I was involved, after the war had started, with a project to try to camouflage the plume of steam coming from the coke ovens. They did have some camouflage paintwork. They tried to paint dazzle patterns on the cooling towers, for instance. In one case they had an asbestos garage and it was used for storing inflammable liquids. On the end of that building they painted a cow to make it look like pastoral country. But I was there one night while I was with the research people at Hartburn and each of us in turn was called upon to do a tour of duty at the works themselves because some research was going on at Billingham. It involved material that was only available from the Billingham pipelines. Some of the people who were working right through the war at this semi-technical plant complained that, 'It wasn't really fair that you lads are sitting there in peace and comfort at Hartburn and we're exposed to the danger of air raids.' They were just on the fringe of the factory. So each of us, in turn, had to do a tour from seven at night. Just spending the night there. Going straight to Billingham at five o'clock when work finished and staying on till eight next morning. It was a morale booster.

(Kenneth Warne, 1922-1968)

The company had started what they called the LDV, Local Defence Volunteers. Dad's Army. In at the start. No uniform. All we had was an armband LDV and they wanted volunteers. A friend suggested to me at the time, he said, 'Well, we'll have to join, Jim, because you know you should join.' I said to him, 'You'll be ideal just coming out of the International Brigade and the experience.' He was an experienced soldier. He'd been in Spain in the International Brigade and he was a brigade commander on an anti-tank battery from Russia. I said to him, 'You'll come in handy,' and he made a remark to me that puzzled me at the time. He said, 'If they'll have me.' I said, 'Well, what do you mean, "if they'll have me"?'

Visit of King George VI and Queen Elizabeth.

He said, 'Well, you never know.' That sort of thing puzzled me. But I learnt afterwards why. He never joined with me. I joined with other riggers and we had these broomsticks for training and we were put in different squads. You had engineers that were like COs. Somehow or other I got made into a corporal. One day a week we hadn't to go home, we used to stop and stay the night. If you were working over you had to get a chit from the engineer to excuse you from going on duty because you were working over till eight o'clock. But then you rejoined your unit after you'd worked over. I was never in the Home Guard at Billingham when they had uniforms but I was there when they took our broomsticks off us and they gave us all Remington rifles, American rifles. I think they were used in the American Civil War because they were that ancient. Then we got one machine-gun that was water-cooled. You had to carry a tank of water with you and put the tube in. We also had a Browning automatic rifle. But I was in charge that night. It would be New Year forty-one. I was in charge which gave me the officer's office. With all the correspondence, confidential papers which I went to peruse through and I found something out where ordinary crooks and their names and where they come from. I came across my friend and went along and it said, 'An active communist vetoed by the Stockton Police.' Here we are, we've been chased out of France, we were on the bones of our backside and we have here an experienced soldier and he was vetoed by the Stockton Police because he was an active communist.

(Jimmy Cutter, 1940-1978)

Beginning of the war, I can remember, they had a shelter built and we were invited to go down because Lord Fleck had his mother living with him then. She was a little old lady from Scotland and we used to go down. I remember leaving our poor dog at home. We used to leave him and make our way down in the woods to the shelter. Things that I can remember about that were the mosquitoes. You'd hear them buzzing around. But afterwards we got a shelter of our own so we didn't go down theirs.

(Winn Williams, daughter of ICI employee)

Damage

At eleven o'clock that night, I wasn't in bed fortunately, but I was preparing for bed when I heard the air raid sirens further away before our factory air raid siren sounded. So I was ready and at about a minute or two past eleven the bombs started to fall and by that time we were all in the shelter and the bombs fell all around. At that time the Main Offices were still there and the labs were still there and there were other buildings and there was a cricket field close beside the works. Bombs fell there about twelve yards away from the shelter and pieces of bomb were thrown out all over. The shelter was so many feet into the ground and covered with earth on top.

(Kenneth Warne, 1922-1968)

But one of the times during the war at Billingham before I went over to Nylon, there was a big raid on the Billingham factory. With incendiaries and high explosive because one high explosive had dropped on one of the conveyor belts that went from plant to plant and destroyed it. There was a load of incendiary bombs spread throughout the factory. Where the ropeways were, across the road, there was a big net. Well, a lot of incendiaries had dropped on the net and hadn't exploded and we had the job of climbing up there and pushing them off to the floor. We didn't know whether they'd exploded or not but they hadn't gone off. One incendiary that had gone off, to the relief of some of the store managers, had burned the stores out and all their books. You can imagine a lot of skulduggery had been going on there.

(Jimmy Cutter, 1940-1978)

The only severe bombing that I could ever remember as seeing taking place during the night was the Instrument Workshops. It was not devastated but it was very, very badly damaged. But all the glass work and all the need for ventilation and so forth was blacked out, was painted over. The Heinkel bombers used to come up the river and use the river as a means of finding ICI and other steelworks and various other people that they had in mind for their target.

(Mansell Shotton, 1942-1984)

Aerial view of smoke over Billingham Site taken by the RAF in 1939.

War work

I didn't work on any of the research projects to do with the war really. There were people working on very secret work to do with the atomic bomb. But I was not in that and contact with their colleagues was vigorously discouraged. They had a section which they called 'Tube Alloys' which was a camouflage name. Everybody who knew it, knew that it was working with uranium and so on but the rest didn't know.

(Kenneth Warne, 1922-1968)

We were directed into industry. They were supposed to be related to the war effort but you know it was almost as if you were fighting the next war rather than the one you were in. One of the things we were working on was torpedo propellants. If you had wanted to develop torpedoes with the kind of propellants which would operate the thing, without leaving a trail of bubbles on the top so you could see where it was coming from, you would have to build a large new plant to make them. You wouldn't have finished that by the time the war ended. So in a sense there was a slightly unreal atmosphere. (Alf Rout, 1940-1977)

In 1944 the war was still on and the RAF had a place on the Ammonia Works. For the barrage-balloons, they used to have all their (hydrogen) bottles. They used to come in there. They used to fill them up and take them all over the country.

(Tom Boumphey, 1944-1987)

During the war years when my father was with ICI, the company used to supply them with Dexalin capsules which contained vitamins A and D and my father was actually working away over in the Lake District at the time because they moved everybody over there away from Teesside. So he used to bring these Dexalin capsules home for my mother to give myself and brother and sister. We used to have one every day with our midday meal and boost up your immune system and everything.

(Patricia Whyman, 1957-1964)

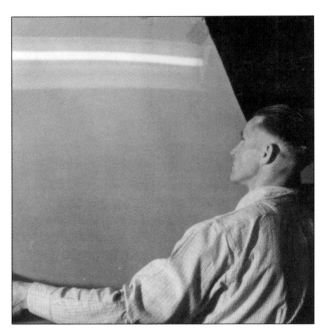

Inspecting Perspex sheet.

Women workers

The very first time was during the war, 1942 and I was in the Perspex Department and we were rolling Perspex. We just went into this big room and there were sheets of the Perspex and it was heating like a grill. One girl was at one side and I was at the other with big long poles and when it got hot enough we had to press. When you think about the technology now where a machine will come down, press it just like that with all the corrugated sheeting ready. We had to roll it tight onto the iron and it was very, very hard.

(Pearl Hall, 1942-1944; 1958-1986)

I was directed there during the war. I was an only child and I had an interview with the Ministry of whatever it was called and my mother came too. I was asked which of the forces I would go into and I said the WRNS. I could have gone into the WRNS with my qualifications with a commission but my mother said, 'Oh, no.' So they said, 'Right, you'll be directed into industry.' She was horrified when she knew I was directed to ICI Billingham.

(Jean Owen, 1941-1945)

I was an instrument artificer. I looked after all the instruments in the plants: flow meters, recorders, temperature gauges. The flow meters had charts on which recorded the flow. First thing on a morning I had to make sure that the chart was working. There was a little pen and the chart went round and the pen recorded the flow. So I had to make sure that they were all working properly and there was plenty of ink in the pens. That was my first job. We were just there if anything went wrong they would send for you. You knew everyone. The men were all friendly. I used to get a nice cup of tea when they had their break. But there was mercury in (the flow meters) and sometimes I'd change the mercury. Nobody ever told me it was poisonous. My wedding ring went white and I had to send it to the jeweller's to get cleaned a couple of times. I had to go to the workshops for one job and one of the young men that worked there, an apprentice, made me a wedding ring so I left mine at home and wore that one. I did have an apprentice working with me and I did say I didn't want to work with him any more. It was a shame really. He got a bit familiar one day and so I thought, 'No.' He was alright, you know, nothing happened. He went and worked with someone else. I'll tell you the one thing I was disappointed about. After the war they had a centenary or something from ICI and they invited the apprentice of the year but they never ever did anything. They just, 'Well,

Women at war, brush hands in 1942.

you're finished now,' and you got your wages and that was it. They did say I could go and work at ICI any time if I wanted to but that was it. We never had a little celebration. We just went and that was it. We came and we went and I thought it would have been nice if we could have had a little get-together.

(Audrey Fryatt, 1942-1945)

But during the war they had a lot of female mates. You used to have the hard-cased women in the hard jobs. Down the coke ovens, they were really tough, those women and especially in the bag part of CCF. They used to have women there but that was after the war as well. But during the war the fitters had mates, women mates, and they had a lot of fitters' mates diluted into fitters during the war. Some of those mates were better than the fitters they worked with because they knew the job.

(Jimmy Cutter, 1940-1978)

When the war started we were off work for seven weeks. Glorious weather. Seven weeks' paid holiday because we couldn't go to work until they'd got air raid shelters prepared. We were moving out to Elmwood in Hartburn.

That was the ICI place during the war. They had various places all over. There's one in Yarm and one in Norton and Newton. They all had different departments. But you couldn't go to the place until the air raid shelters were up and at first we worked in Redwing Lane for a while. I used to have to go into the library in the mornings in the old Main Offices that are knocked down, aren't they? Get the books out that were required for the day. I had a list of what was wanted and I had to go into the library in the Main Offices and you couldn't put the light on because it wasn't properly blacked out. It was camouflaged but it wasn't blacked out. So I used to have to go into the library and get a large torch and go crawling around the bookshelves and get all the books out for different people. Anybody wanting a book had to put their name down for it and I would get it.

(Bella Burnicle, 1935-1946)

My husband had to go in the Army and we had to be called up and I had to choose between the three forces or the munitions. My husband didn't want me to go in the forces. Because we had a house in Middlesbrough to look after while he was away, I decided on ICI. Well, the ICI was nearer for me because, as I say, we'd got a house off Linthorpe Road and I could cut through to get the bus on Newport Road to ICI. I went into an interview and I wanted to be in the Plastics Department making all the lovely plastics. They put me into the Sodium and Salt Plant. They took me in there and I thought it was going into hell because all the men were dressed as Ku Klux Klan. They were all in white and they were covered up and they had these pokers and they were poking these big pots of fire. These pots were exploding every now and again and I thought, 'Oh, where have they brought me to?' I asked for a day job and they gave me cyanide [plant]. So you filled trays of cyanide. You got boxes, bags of cyanide flakes and you put the bags of flakes of cyanide on the tray, these tin trays and you lifted them into the ovens and put them there. But after about two or three months I got a rash on my feet. So I went to the doctor's and he said, 'Go and tell them you'll have to have a change.' So they changed me. Then I asked for another change and they put me onto the railway station, onto the railway trucks, filling the railway trucks with the squashed tins, of all things. Yes, recycling. The women were lifting the tins, these boxes of squashed tins. I did that for a week and I was so fed up I thought, 'This is like being in punishment.' So I saw one of the bosses. I stopped him and I said, 'I want a change.' Anyway, he got me a nice job in a hut as you come in the gates. Everybody who worked in the plant had to have a gas mask. So you'd give the gas masks to the men who worked in the plant and then they used to bring them back to have them changed. I worked there until I finished.

(Stella Felce, 1942-1943)

I changed my job when my husband went abroad. I couldn't see him or anything. He was just home for the odd weekend. I decided then I would go to work at ICI and get myself a job and save up for when Ron came home and then we could go and buy furniture because before that furniture was all on coupons. I was on the Water Gas Plant. On the floor there was a big round hole and it was covered by iron. The top went on. But every so long you had to take a

measurement of the stuff that was in and it used to measure up on the plant. Then if you needed any more fuel you would just have to ring a bell and there used to be a little tractor thing going right round the top. You just had to stand there if you needed more fuel.

(Dorothy Goodwin, 1941-1946)

Had the choice of Land Army, enlisting, or ICI. Went to Billingham on spec and was given a job straight away. The wage was four pounds a week - a fortune. Training given by the foreman. 'Push this lever, watch that gauge, if it develops a funny noise, run like hell.'

(Doris Jolly, 1939-1945)

American and Canadian airmen would sometimes visit to see where their cockpits were started. Their visits were regarded with great excitement.

(Jessie Smith, 1942-1946)

Telephonists in the manual exchange in the old Main Offices.

Chapter
11

'No longer was there a job for life' Competition and decline

Until the beginning of the 1960s production at ICI continued to increase and markets for key products made at Billingham, such as ammonia, methanol and fertilizers, expanded. This was good news for the approximately 16,000 employees then based at the Billingham Site. However, there were problems looming on the horizon.

Increasingly, ICI was facing competition from North American and other European firms who had expanded their production in wartime. This increased capacity was forcing prices down. There were two key factors that had to be addressed: other firms were using more advanced and cost-effective technology and they had better productivity.

Some of the technology at Billingham was falling behind its major international competitors. For example, ammonia production was reliant on coal but this was not cost-effective. The coke ovens and other plants which had been built in the 1930s were coming to the end of their productive life. To compete effectively with those producers who were using oil as a cheaper alternative, the Billingham Site began to use naphtha as a feedstock in the ammonia plants in the early sixties and then switched to natural gas later in the decade. They also built large single-stream plants to update the ammonia production technology. This cut production costs by half. A more efficient process for producing methanol was also introduced in this period and new plants manufacturing such products as urea and Nitram were developed. But many of these technological developments had an impact on the number of staff needed to run the plants and by 1965 the number of employees at Billingham was reduced to less than 14,000. As uneconomic plants continued to be closed and more efficient plants opened,

staffing levels continued to fall. By 1972 the total number of employees had dropped again to just over 10,000 and that figure had fallen to about 6,500 by the mid 1980s.

Competition in the fertilizer business became more intense when a Norwegian chemical company, Norsk Hydro, bought Fisons' fertilizer business. ICI had been supplying ammonia to Fisons and had been able to keep production costs low because of the preferential price of gas they had negotiated with British Gas. However, the Norwegian firm were able to produce large amounts of ammonia, had access to supplies of cheap North Sea gas, and quickly increased their share of the fertilizer market.

Under pressure from these changes, ICI continued to develop new technological processes but these also potentially threatened the commercial viability of the Billingham Site. For instance, in 1982 a new process for producing ammonia that used about 30 per cent less natural gas was brought on stream. But this could only function in new plants and these new plants were being built on other sites. The other problem for Billingham was the changing commercial strategy of the company. Increasingly, ICI focused on producing speciality chemicals and in 1983 formed a new Speciality Chemicals Division. Continued decline in demand for fertilizer and competition from other low-cost suppliers worsened the position at Billingham. In 1986 ICI dramatically cut the price of its products, closed plants and initiated a programme of redundancies. The output of fertilizers fell dramatically and in 1997 the fertilizer plants at Billingham were sold to Terra Industries. This was in line with ICI's decision to reorganise its business portfolio by acquiring speciality chemical companies and disposing of its bulk chemicals business.

The company did try to soften the impact of these changes. In the early 1980s a resettlement group was established in Agricultural Division to provide information and practical advice for workers whose jobs were threatened. Over the next few years, resettlement activities increased as the rate of plant closure quickened. A job shop opened and employees were offered counselling services, training in interview techniques and information about self-employment. In the late 1980s ICI established Belasis Hall Technology Park to encourage the development of small chemical or technology companies. These policies did deflect criticism from ICI and helped limit the damage to the image of the company in this period of change and decline.

Despite these initiatives, this was obviously a challenging period for ICI employees and those who had any interest in its survival on Teesside. This is eloquently expressed in the extracts that follow.

Low productivity

When I started on circulation there were nineteen men, one on every machine. On north injection there were five people, in south injection there were eight people because of more leaks there. Four of those people were mostly running around looking for drums to stick under leaks. But when I left three and a half men were looking after those three plants which had twenty-eight people working when I first went. It was down to three and a half looking after the lot and no supervisors. Automation without any doubt. Automation and study of men's methods of working, WSA, as it was called. Work study that was the main thing that shifted. To give a very clear indication of that, there was actually a chargehand and four men there in K pump house. When automation came and the wash plants were on automatic they didn't need anybody to look after them really. Needed somebody to go and take the readings and make sure everything was checked and not anybody to change the valves over or anything.

(Fred Moody, 1946-1982)

In the early sixties, there was over-manning. Work practices were funny. When you're there and there are thousands of people, it doesn't dawn on you that working practices were so bad. But nowadays, I go to work and whatever engineering problems come up is mine. But in those days everyone was designated so if you were a plumber that was your job. Nobody else dare touch your job. They'd have got their fingers chopped off if they were caught. My boss came in one day and he says, 'Do you want to work Sunday, it's double-time?' So there was a pump wanted changing and they needed a fitter to change the pump - one person. So when I arrived there, I had to have a fitter's mate so I had a labourer with me and because we were out my boss came out so there was three of us. But because it was connected to an electrical motor they had to have an electrician out to disconnect the motor because I couldn't touch it. And because the electrician was out he had to have an electrician's mate. And because they were out they had to have their foremen out so there were three of them. And because it was a big pump you had to have two riggers out. And because they were out you had to have the riggers' boss, so there was three of them. And you had to have a crane driver. Honest. I remember it well because I counted it up and there were actually eleven men there. But it wasn't just ended there because of the paperwork you had to go through, all the estimating work and planning work. You had massive ICI offices and all the paperwork was filled out for a job like that in triplicate. There was a pink sheet, a green sheet, a white sheet - something like that - and each sheet went to different offices for them to do the paperwork on it. So there were people employed there as well. They were grossly over-manned.

(Dave Peacock, 1960-1972)

Greater competition

In ICI I didn't give a moment's thought to ICI's competitors and I think that was a huge weakness. It did not distil in its employees that commercial awareness that I think is necessary in any organisation. It was not a company where you got people coming in from the outside and saying, 'Why are you doing it that way, isn't there another way to do it?' That has only happened within the last decade, by which time the company was transformed. Perhaps it would have been better if there were people asking those questions. So you got this oligarchy running the company who'd been in the company thirty, forty years to get to that sort of situation, who'd been brought up to believe that half of the world was red and that was where ICI sold all its products all the time without too much competition. Now it had to come to terms with Europe and had to come to terms with changing competitive conditions in the market place at home with our entering into the EU, as well as the Norwegian issue which was particularly relevant to Billingham.

(John Robinson, 1969-1989)

In the fifties and sixties we were in a dominant position but the business became more international. We became exposed to competition from abroad and it was quite clear that we had to cut the cost of production. Now we were succeeding in doing that, we were succeeding by developing a new technology and this is where ICI had tremendous strength. It was an intellectual powerhouse, we recruited just the first class honours of every technical discipline that you could have. It was quite unique, the capability was enormous and it was that capability that enabled us to develop new processes. As we developed the new processes the costs came down but these new processes required a fraction of the labour. So this is where in striving to maintain our position in the world we just simply had to move in that direction and that meant, of course, that no longer was there a job for life. No longer was there the security that prevailed in the fifties and the sixties. This is where the alignment of interest had changed. This was one of the tasks that we had to do; we had to bring home that reality. Now just to put that in context, I had

the opportunity to go to the United States and where we did a productivity comparison and I went with the man who subsequently became the chairman of the division. We went to major manufacturers. It was very nice and it surprised me how open they were about sharing their organisation. We were able to compare organisations and we came back with the rather sobering conclusion that for every three or four people that we had, they had one. And we even found one ammonia plant where for every six people we had, they had one. We had no longer moved from a domestic market, we had moved to an international market - or we were moving. That movement, the effect of that became more and more extreme and so there was just an imperative. If we didn't do it we wouldn't survive and in the end we didn't survive. And leaving the labour costs aside, ammonia plants were being built out in the Middle East and they were being built, metaphorically, on top of an oil well. They got their natural gas for nothing. We had to pay for natural gas from the North Sea and the Government was taking something like 70 per cent tax from it. So the dice was loaded against the business and what we were embarked on was a struggle to maintain our viability.

(George McKinlay, 1957-1985)

Unprofitable plants and processes

ICI Billingham was becoming insufficiently profitable in many ways. It wasn't giving ICI its expected return on capital and it was quite clear that an important element in this was that the ICI Site was highly labour-intensive. If you look at the horde of miners underground and the large numbers of people working on things like [ammonium]sulphate and so forth, these were highly labour-intensive and you could get out of this by changing the style of processes at Billingham altogether. One way of doing it was to get rid of the anhydrite basis altogether and before I went there they had looked at this problem in pieces. Should we turn the old Sulphuric Acid Plant into a sulphur burning plant so that you don't have all this cement business hanging around you? You could get rid of the anhydrite from the Sulphuric Acid

Plant in a fairly straightforward fashion and this would take you out of the cement business to a large extent but not entirely because it was based partly on cement coming from the Sulphuric Acid Plant and partly on chalk from the Nitro-Chalk Plant. The Sulphate Plant was the next big thing that one would like to get out of altogether. Ammonium sulphate was the main nitrogen fertilizer used by not only the British farmer but many farmers around the world. But the sulphate part was no good to the soil at all. The sulphate part was merely something there to hang on to the ammonia which is a volatile gas. There's another kind of chemical, ammonium nitrate which has got nitrogen in both halves. Ammonium sulphate has got what? Twenty-odd per cent of nitrogen in it, ammonium nitrate has got 35 per cent in it. So you got more than one and half times as much in carriage, packing and all the rest of it. But there were difficulties about changing over to ammonium nitrate and there were many people reluctant to do it on that basis alone. But, on the other hand, it would have been a step into what was then the modern era. So what I was doing was promoting a scheme for shutting down all the anhydrite-based activities, altogether all at once. And you could make quite a good case for that. I was well aware that I was dealing in a matter that would put a lot of people out of work. On the other hand you could say I was dealing with a project that would keep a lot more people in work than would have been the case if they had simply shut down their fertilizer activities altogether. So, in a sense, I was doing a lot of people a lot of harm but I was also protecting a lot of people from something a lot worse.

(Alf Rout, 1940-1977)

That's when it started to become really quite serious and it started in the seventies and I think it was the central feature of the eighties. The eighties certainly were all about costs, cost reduction, about efficiency improvement, about it's a very competitive world. You know Russians and Poles were importing material into England to compete with us for the first time. It changed and changed in a pretty big way and particularly in the eighties. That was when really fundamental changes with reducing the number of plants or reducing the amount of manpower on the Site, contracting out some of the activities that were contracted out - that's when it really got into the full swing because the competitive world was very, very tough at that time. That's when you started to get a sense that corporate headquarters weren't too sure that they wanted to be for another fifty years in the sort of things that we were doing, the heavy chemicals. So Billingham was about ammonia and fertilizer and methanol, thousands of tons per day. So was Wilton and over that period the sense developed that Millbank weren't really very interested in that. They liked pharmaceuticals and they liked paints and they liked these mysterious things called specialties. As far as we were concerned they didn't make any money and nobody knew what they were anyway and it sounded like a bunch of crap to us. The message, whether it was intended or not, started to arrive that 'them at headquarters' in London weren't really behind these sorts of things. And that's a very, very powerful message. I mean imagine your father saying to you, 'I'm sorry, you might be my son but I don't particularly like you. I'm not very bothered if I never see you again!'

(Keith Farmery, 1970-2000)

Impact on workforce

There was nothing wrong with the ICI. What was wrong was the people that ran it, the little plastic men that came at the end – when the chairman of ICI was an accountant and that's all he was. He was just there to get rid of ICI for as much money as he could. There was no feeling of men or anything like that. That all disappeared.

(Barry Dunnill, 1956-1994)

Unfortunately, gas prices went up enormously during the seventies and eighties, and eventually British Gas actually went to arbitration with ICI and forced the gas price up, which really started the demise of Agricultural Division. The gas price went up, fertilizer prices in the world were not high and eventually Billingham started to lose money and the things I got involved with were to actually reduce numbers and that's the time when I'd moved to the works and effectively we had to be cost efficient or the Billingham Division would lose more and more money. The sort of things we got into involved actually reducing numbers and that was done always in ICI terms without redundancy. It was always done with early retirement or ways of helping people to find other jobs. We spent enormous amounts of time, effort, money helping people to find new jobs outside of ICI, inside ICI, wherever we could find them. ICI itself was still a large company and therefore we could actually use other divisions. But, because the people were locally based, it was very difficult to move people. If they were prepared to move they were given all the help possible to actually help them move. But, in fact, people had their own local area. One of the major problems we actually had was getting job resettlement within the locality of Teesside. There were early retirement packages for people over 50 years old. We did a lot of novel things with people such as seconding them to other organisations to help them move, because one of the psychological problems you had with people who'd worked at somewhere like Billingham for a long time was actually getting them to see that there is a life outside.

(George Cooke, 1972-2001)

There were no redundancies unless they wished to take redundancies, of course. The monthly staff, the majority of them, were re-deployed but some of them weren't and unfortunately there were one or two people who were given redundancy payments. Then I was involved in this job scheme - this job shop - to try and get people into other employment, one of whom I can recall was a chappie who was assistant foreman. He came back to visit us and he'd gone to Australia on the strength of some work we'd done and he got a job with the Dulux people in Adelaide in Australia. He was the southern area representative for all of Australia for Dulux, so he did very well out of it.

(George McGee, 1951-1985)

The first thing they did, they came round and said, 'Look, there's no official redundancies, ICI doesn't want any.' We were told by a works engineer and a shop steward. They said, 'But if anybody wants it, just go in and ask and they'll give you it.' So a few people were pondering it and a few people went in and asked what the need was. There were certain people they'd say, 'Can you come in the engineer's office regarding employment?' When they went in they said, 'Right, here's your record for the last few years, your time-keeping is absolutely shocking, it's atrocious.' They'd said nothing for years, just given them an inch and they've taken a mile. So they said, 'We want you to volunteer to take redundancy and leave.' 'I don't want to go, I've got a mortgage, I've got kids, I don't want to be redundant.' 'It's up to you. We're suggesting you volunteer but if you don't, the very next time you're late for work or you have a day off, you'll be sacked and you'll get nothing. So we want you to volunteer with your dole.' I think that was a deliberate ploy to let people put themselves in that position and by doing that, of course, they've got rid of the wasters and the dead wood.

(Dave Peacock, 1960-1972)

Outsourcing was where ICI was selling off parts of the company to other firms and, in my case, I went with the computer section. The interested party was Philips Electronics and they had a sub-division called Origin that managed all the Philips computing business, and they were in the business of acquiring firms by then, so they bought the entire computing section lock, stock and barrel and it all went over. So I was already a bit peeved at the fact the company was doing that. But what really annoyed me was that the head of the computing section at the time, who swore to us that he was coming with us, at the last minute was kept back by ICI. We all felt that had he come with us he would have provided some sort of continuity within the new organisation. But we all went in without a head then, if you like. Our boss suddenly was a man who worked for the other firm. And, of course, he had his own ideas and he didn't understand how ICI were. Because any big company has a way of working and you get used to it, don't you? I mean one of the things that always impressed me about ICI is what I call this civil service. You could pick a phone up. You had a problem with your pay chit. Pick a phone up and speak to someone and they would sort it out. If you had a personnel issue, you knew who to ring.

Suddenly all that had gone. That basket of protection and wraparound comfort, it had all gone and it was never replaced. We weren't to know what ICI's motivation for doing it was. But people like me who up to the time of the transfer out, twenty-six years' service, felt we deserved better than that. That we had given a lot of loyal company time and it didn't seem to be taken into account. I know they tried to protect our interests, to protect the pension fund. There's probably no company could have done more when we were actually outsourced to protect our interests but that doesn't get away from the fact you've worked for a big company that you felt loyal to and a lot of people like me with families had suddenly just been told, 'Off you go, no use for you any more.'

(Eric Collins, 1970-1976)

But they died out - the smokers. ICI went all cost conscious. They wouldn't pay anything out. They stopped smokers, they stopped everything like this. Post 1980 when it all changed. Before that it was like everything happened. As you look in the old ICI magazines it was reported in there if somebody was sick. In the ICI magazine it was, 'We offer our condolences'. All that disappeared. I would say from 1990 I found it was all in vain. I thought, 'Well, what am I doing here? What have I done here? They don't want people dedicated, they just want like a contractor. They just want you as a contractor. If you don't turn up tomorrow we'll get somebody else.' That's how I felt and I felt let down at the end.

(Barry Dunnill, 1956-1994)

Methanol Plant.

Chapter 12

'A very fine company' Final thoughts

I hear things have changed considerably now but in those days they were like a big family. There were fallouts and whatnot but generally speaking we all got on very well together. I enjoyed every moment. Because I've enjoyed my life, I looked forward to going to work which a lot of people don't.

(John Pape, 1948-1991)

I think ICI was a very fine company for the fact that there were very few difficult personal relationships. There were very few people who were badly treated. We were very big and we were all very proud to work for it.

(Robin Cook, 1961-1993)

I had a good time at ICI. It was hard work and we worked to strict rules. But you felt that you were treated by everybody as a real person and I was promoted to a job I really enjoyed.

(Dennis Duggan, 1959-1998)

You just felt cocooned by ICI. That's how I felt all my working life.

(Linda Flintoff, 1964-1976)

It was this benevolent attitude, the philosophy of looking after people and treating people with respect. Rewarding people well. They paid well. They looked after their people well. People were simply looked after. There was security and because there was security and people were treated with respect there was no conflict. There was an alignment of interests. That changed.

(George McKinlay, 1957-1985)

I thought it was a brilliant firm to work for. Like anywhere you tend to have rose-tinted specs but I know I was very happy, very happy virtually in every job that I did and I always felt I was encouraged by management to try and better myself. Encouraged to do things and encouraged to push yourself that bit further. I always found it very good in that way.

(Eric Collins, 1970-1976)

They were superb employers. It was very easy to be a doctor at ICI. In my thirty years with them, never had any problem with going and saying, 'This is a man who is very ill. He needs this, he needs that, how can we help him?' And it was easy. They made my job very easy in that respect.

(David Bryson, 1962-1992)

The positives were security. You went to ICI and they had good benefits. It was security, reasonable regular wages. They'd got a good system of work, protective clothing, all things like that. And I suppose the camaraderie because most people came from the same area like Billingham, probably people who lived in the same street. So it was like a community within a community. Those are the sort of things that stick in your mind. But, you know, in essence, it was a pleasure to go to work in those days.

(Dennis Carroll, 1952-1979)

There were some really good people. It was a challenging company, intellectually it was an exciting company to work for because there were a lot of bright people around and when we had some issues to deal with it was a pleasure to debate and discuss.

(John Robinson, 1969-1989)

It was a good employer because it could afford to be and it could afford to be because it was in all sorts of monopolies. So if they treated their employees well, they could pass it on to the customer without a problem. It's important to remember this feature of ICI, a very good employer. But it was a very good employer because the structure of world chemical industry into which it fitted, enabled it to be.

(Alf Rout, 1940-1977)

We had nice company, nice fellowship and nice companionship.

(Gladys Lindwood, 1938-1978)

Most people knew everybody. You knew so many people. It was all worthwhile. You enjoyed yourself.

(George Morgan, 1952-1982)

Work was not a place to avoid.

(Alf Illingworth, 1952-1969)

I was told that ICI was a very secure place. You had a job for life there and, as it happens, I was there for life.

(William Hudson, 1951-1990)

I was always thankful for them teaching me skills. I didn't only go to the college to learn typing. We did Geography and English and that sort of thing. It furthered my education.

(Barbara Illingworth, 1951-1956)

It was fantastic working for ICI.

(Anne Tuffs, 1955-1967)

We were in a small office and we were all very friendly and managers and engineers and superintendents from the factory all came to the office. Everybody was very friendly.

(Doreen Sell, 1947-1959)

'How secure is this job of mine going to be?' He said, 'Oh, ICI'll be here long after you've gone.' 'Oh,' I said, 'that sounds good.'

(Gordon Blacklock, 1953-1981)

ICI was stamped through people like in a stick of rock.

(George McKinlay, 1957-1985)

One of the happiest times of my life was at ICI. I couldn't speak more highly of the management and I'm not just being patriotic. They really were very good to speak to and they would listen. And do you know I think they learnt from us as well. They learnt from us and if only I had my time all over again I would choose to go back. Wonderful! I wish I could have it over again.

(Pearl Hall, 1942-1944; 1958-1986)

The 'Pruteen' Plant opened in 1979 was the first diversification towards bioengineering.

Appendix 1

Contributors and their dates of service at ICI Billingham

Employees

Maurice Benson, 1967-1999
Gordon Blacklock, 1953-1981
Sean Booth, 1974-1994
Tom Boumphey, 1944-1987
Gill Bowness, 1956-1991
Anthony Brennan, 1955-1985
David Bryson, 1962-1992
Stan Buglass, 1937-1980
Bella Burnicle, 1935-1946
Austin Carney, 1966-1997
Dennis Carroll, 1952-1979
June Challenger, 1949-1950; 1969-1985
Eric Christie, 1953-1983
Eric Collins, 1970-1976
Robin Cook, 1961-1993
George Cooke, 1972-2001
Frank Curry, 1969-1985
Jimmy Cutter, 1940-1978
Brian Deans, 1957-1993
Robert de Wardt, 1957-1981
Ronald Dowd, 1970-1990
Dennis Duggan, 1959-1998
Barry Dunnill, 1956-1994
Keith Farmery, 1970-2000
Stella Felce, 1942-1943
Linda Flintoff, 1964-1976
Donald Foster, 1938-1960s
Ellen Foster, 1950-1985
Audrey Fryatt, 1942-1945
Brenda Fuller, 1963-1967
Edward George, 1958-1988
Dorothy Goodwin, 1941-1945
Thomas Green, 1953-1991
Pearl Hall, 1942-1944; 1958-1986
Stanley Hawksfield, 1950-1978
Bill (Ginger) Hawthorne, 1953-1964
Bill Henderson, 1965-1971
Margaret Hopper, 1957-1961
William Hudson, 1951-1990
Barbara Illingworth, 1951-1956
Alf Illingworth, 1952-1969
Harry Irvine, 1951-1973
Doris Jolly, 1941-1943
Gladys Lindwood, 1938-1978

Anthony Lynn, 1945-1989
Ray Marriner, 1949-1985
George McKinlay, 1957-1985
Patricia McNerney, 1945-1949
Jean Miller, 1952-1954
Don Miller, 1943-1971
Betty Mitchell, 1957-1982
Fred Moody, 1946-1982
Robert Moran, 1966-1993
George Morgan, 1952-1982
Gwen Mountain, 1956-1960
Rita Nicholson, 1948-1966
Eugene (Hughie) Norman, 1958-2005
Jean Owen, 1941-1945
Dennis Oxley, 1955-1985
John Francis Pape, 1948-1991
Dave Peacock, 1960-1972
Julian Phillips, 1956-1985
John Robinson, 1969-1989
Brian Rodgers, 1957-1987
Alf Rout, 1940-1977
Doreen Sell, 1947-1959
Mansell Shotton, 1942-1984
Roy Simpson, 1958-1999
Jessie Smith, 1942-1946
William Smith, 1964-1998
Christopher Snowdon, 1974-2005
Rita Stafford, 1961-1991
Jim Steedman, 1946-1987
David Sutheran, 1978-1982
Mike Thompson, 1952-1990
Bob Tucker, 1937-1949
Anne Tuffs, 1955-1967
Doug Wallace, 1957-2000
Kenneth Warne, 1922-1968
Patricia Whyman, 1957-1964
Allan Wilderspin, 1953-1955
Ron Wilson, 1960-1989
Bill Wright (Industrial Chaplain), 1959-1992

Relatives of employees

Lilian Benson
Anne Boyes
Shirley Cooke
Winn Williams

Appendix

2

How ICI was organised

This organisation chart is a snapshot of the mid 1960s. There were continual changes until the complete reorganisation of 1986 with the creation of ICI Chemicals & Polymers.

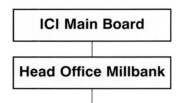

ICI Main Board

Head Office Millbank

Divisions with a Board (but without legal responsibility as separate companies).
Typically a chairman, two deputy chairmen and 12 directors.

AGRICULTURAL DIVISION

PRODUCTION WORKS	**FUNCTIONAL DEPARTMENTS**
(Each works was divided into plants some of which were joined into sections.)	(Each department was divided into groups which, in turn, were divided into sections.)
Gas & Power Water Gas Plant Power Station **Ammonia** Ammonia Nitric Acid **Products** Fertilizers Industrial Chemicals **Engineering Works** **Research Works** (later merged with Research Dept) **Commercial Works** Storage Packing Physical Transport (later merged with Distribution Dept. to become Distribution & Services Works)	**Fertilizer Sales** **Industrial Products Sales** **Building Products Sales** **Research** (later R&D, latterly R&T) **Accounts** **Engineering** **Distribution** **Management Services** **Planning & Co-ordination** **Safety** **Medical Staff** **Labour** (later Personnel) **Secretary's**

How the Billingham Site was organised

Appendix 3

In 1931 ICI created a new subsidiary ICI Fertilizer and Synthetic Products Ltd to run the ammonia based business. At the same time the newer Cassel Works on its South Site was transferred to General Chemicals Ltd which had its headquarters at Runcorn, Merseyside.

A major ICI reorganisation in 1944 was intended to put the company in a position to seize the opportunities of post-war growth. A series of quasi-independent divisions* was formed, but these were no longer actual companies as separate legal entities. Nonetheless they all had a board with a chairman and directors. The ammonia and oil businesses at Billingham became Billingham Division.

Again, Cassel Works was separate and came under General Chemicals Division (from 1962 Mond Division) until its transfer to Agricultural Division in 1981.

In 1958 Oil Works, and Billingham's interests in the olefines and related plants at the newer, larger Wilton Site south of the River Tees, were hived off to form Heavy Organic Chemicals Division (HOC), later renamed to Petrochemicals Division and finally merged to form Petrochemicals and Plastics Division.

Two further divisions acquired small sites at the south end of its Billingham Site. Dyestuffs Division to make nylon, and Plastics Division to make Perspex acrylic sheet from polymer material made at the adjoining Cassel Works. Later, Nylon Works was transferred to Plastics Division.

Also on the eastern flank of the Site ICI helped to set up British Titan Products (BTP) which produced white pigment for paints. ICI originally held a third of BTP but subsequently took 100 per cent ownership.

*The original divisions were:

Billingham (from 1964 Agricultural)

Alkali

General Chemicals

Salt

Lime

Dyestuffs } merged in 1962 to form

Plastics } Mond Division

Paints

Leathercloths (later merged with Paints)

Nobel

Later additions were:

Fibres

Plant Protection

Pharmaceuticals

Paints

Appendix 4

Map of Billingham Site c1960

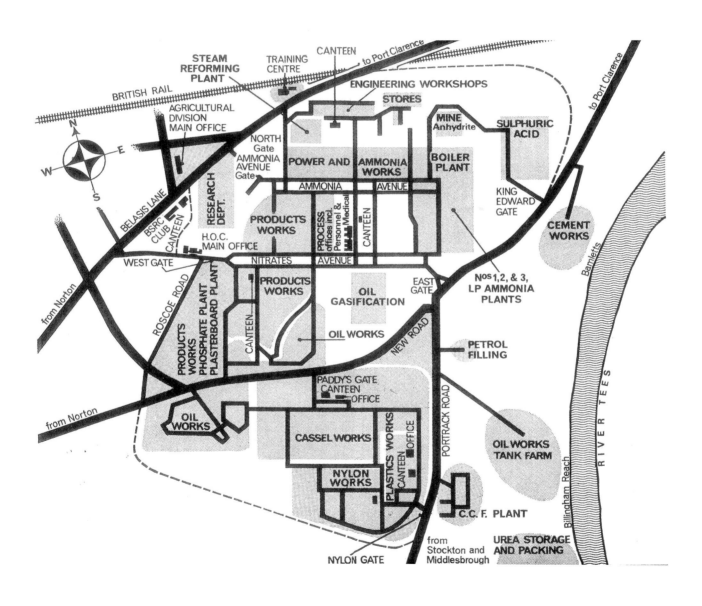

Appendix 5

Map of ICI Billingham and surrounding areas

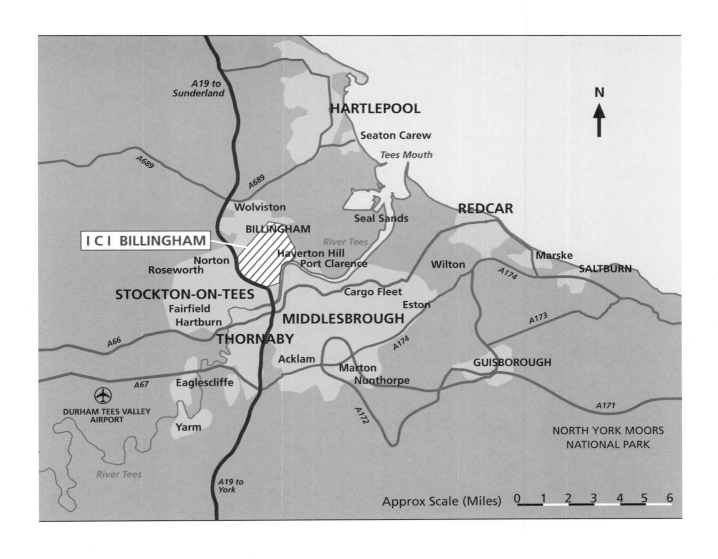

Sodium cell room, Cassel Works.

Lifting new distillation column in Oil Works.

The four steam reformers built in 1962.

Process worker.

North Gate in the 1960s.

The Power Station in 1984 with Ammonia Works in the background.

West Gate bus station and Synthonia cricket field.

The lounge at Norton Hall.

Instruments and staff in the Phenol Plant room.

Audio typists.

Process worker checking instruments.

Gala Day on the Synthonia cricket field.

Working in a Registry.

Telephonists in the manual exchange in the old Main Offices.

The Process Works canteen in the foreground. The camouflage from the war is clearly visible.

Chilton House and West Gate.

Research Department Ladies Football Team at Synthonia football ground in 1971.

Queen opening the Apprentice School in 1957.

At work in the new Process Offices.

Research Party in 1967.